For Caroline

TOURING THE
GIANT'S RIB
A GUIDE TO THE NIAGARA ESCARPMENT

TOURING THE
GIANT'S RIB

A GUIDE TO THE NIAGARA ESCARPMENT

LORINA AND GARY STEPHENS

Stoddart A BOSTON MILLS PRESS BOOK

For Adam and Kelly

Acknowledgements

CREATING THIS BOOK took over our lives for more than a year, although we had been touring the secret places of the escarpment for several years before. And though it consumed much of our time, we would have been unable to complete it with any degree of competence without the help of many people who gave their time and knowledge without any expectation of return. For their assistance we would like to thank Richard Murzin, Darcy Baker, John Winters, Kevin Hawthorne, Peter Robson, Martin Parker, Bob Day, Ian Kirkham, Brian Howard, John Denison, and Barbara Mackenzie.

We are also grateful to the following organizations: Niagara Escarpment Commission, Niagara Peninsula Conservation Authority, Ministry of Natural Resources, Carolinian Canada Committee, Federation of Ontario Naturalists, Credit Valley Conservation Authority, Halton Region Conservation Authority, Hamilton/Wentworth Conservation Authority, Niagara Parks Commission, Grey-Sauble Conservation Authority, Orangeville Public Library, Ojibwe Cultural Foundation, Chippewas of Nawash Band Office, Parks Canada and Nottawasaga Conservation Authority.

Lorina J. Stephens
Gary Stephens
Orangeville, Ontario, 1993

Canadian Cataloguing in Publication Data

Stephens, Lorina J.
 Touring the giant's rib: a guide to the Niagara escarpment

Includes bibliographical references.
ISBN 1-55046-084-6

1. Niagara Escarpment (Ont.) - Guidebooks.
I. Stephens, Gary, 1953- . II. Title.

FC3095.N48S84 1993   917.13'38   C93-093611-6
F1059.N48S84 1993

First published in 1993 by
Stoddart Publishing Co. Limited
34 Lesmill Road
Toronto, Canada
M3B 2T6
(416) 445-3333

A BOSTON MILLS PRESS BOOK
The Boston Mills Press
132 Main Street
Erin, Ontario
N0B 1T0

Winners of the
Heritage Canada
Communications Award

American Association
for State and Local History
Award Winner

Design by Mary Firth
Photographs by Gary Stephens
Printed in Singapore

The publisher gratefully acknowledges the support of the Canada Council, Ontario Ministry of Culture and Communications, Ontario Arts Council, and Ontario Publishing Centre in the development of writing and publishing in Canada.

Front cover: Land bridge at Bruce National Park. *Back cover:* Flowerpot Island, Bruce National Park

Sand dunes at Singing Sands

Contents

Lavender Falls

INTRODUCTION

Called the Giant's Rib, this bony ridge of land rises from Queenston on the Niagara River and retreats into Lake Huron at Tobermory, emerging once again at Manitoulin and St. Joseph islands.

This is the Niagara Escarpment we in Canada know. In fact, the 1,050-kilometre (650-mile) sickle-shaped cuesta (a ridge with a steep face on one side and a gentle slope on the other) begins in the United States, south of Rochester, New York, plunges north through Canada for its bulk and ends at the Door Peninsula in Wisconsin. Of that enormous area, 725 kilometres (450 miles) lie under the protection of the Niagara Escarpment Plan, Canada's first large-scale environmental land-use plan. It is administered through the Ministry of the Environment by the Niagara Escarpment Commission. Recently, the United Nations Education, Scientific and Cultural Organization (UNESCO) designated the Niagara Escarpment a Man and the Biosphere Reserve. This designation recognizes the unique natural features of the escarpment, its ecological importance and the existing land-use regulation program.

It is this Canadian area of the escarpment we hope to reveal to you in all its grandeur, mystery and marvel. Those three qualities are found in the myriad waterfalls that cascade from the escarpment's heights, in the sweeping valleys and gorges and in the abundant wetlands. Recognizing that it would be impossible to cover everything in just one volume, we hope to whet your appetite for your own exploration and discovery.

To set the stage, some information about how this geological formation came to exist will be useful. Between 500 to 300 million years ago, during the Silurian era, vast inland seas advanced and retreated several times, flooding the Precambrian rock. The bay in which the escarpment was formed was centred in Michigan.

As time passed, rivers flowing from the Canadian Shield emptied into the bay. The Canadian Shield, also known as the Laurentian Plateau, is a shield-shaped area of Precambrian rock upon which all other rock formations rest. It runs from Greenland through Labrador and around Hudson Bay. River depositions resulted in large deltas, which, near the shore, were clay. Such clay deposits were eventually pressurized into rock shales. Farther from shore the muddy ooze was colonized by marine creatures. Here the surface water was rich, supporting plankton and other invertebrates. As they died, limestone was formed. At the northern end of the bay, the waters were clearest, and coral reefs grew. Today, those ancient corals can be seen in rock cuts along Highway 6 on the Bruce Peninsula.

Three hundred million years ago the seas retreated for the last time; the sinking process was reversed, leaving the seabed exposed, thousands of metres thick over the Precambrian rock.

What happened next can only be theorized. It is supposed that the outer edge of the basin sprang free from the granite base, thrusting up what was to become the Niagara Escarpment. A hard caprock of dolostone emerged (caused by the bonding of marine limestone and magnesium), under which were successive layers of soft shales and limestones.

Originally farther east than it lies today, the escarpment has receded approximately 80 kilometres (50 miles). The hydraulic forces of frost were one cause of erosion, sapping the underlying limestone and shale until the caprock cracked under its own weight and fell to form the talus slopes, distinguished by rock debris at the foot of cliffs.

The other force was the rush of ancient northeast rivers that carved enormous gorges, much the way the Niagara River carved its way from Lewiston to its present location. Evidence of these mammoth watercourses remains in the harbours of Colpoy's Bay and Owen Sound.

About one million years ago, Pleistocene glaciers advanced and retreated four times, further sculpturing the escarpment and gouging out the Great Lakes.

The effect of the glaciers was twofold. During the advances, the ice sliced off the tops of rises and smoothed the sides of valleys, polishing and scratching bedrock as it travelled. Retreats created the moraines that fan across Ontario, such as those found near Orangeville, Glen Huron and Flesherton. These irregular hills are composed primarily of clay, sand, gravel and boulders, which were carried to the front of the glaciers by flowing ice, and then dumped as the sheets paused in their retreat. In yet other places, the rock of the escarpment was buried under hundreds of metres of glacial silt, evident in the Mono Cliffs and Scott's Falls (or Cannings Falls) areas.

The retreats also caused other fascinating occurrences: drumlins at Sky Lake, now covered in forest; kettles such as Tobermory Bog, which had been an ice lens; eskers of sand

Niagara Gorge

and gravel that had been melt-water streams flowing beneath the ice; shoals of caprock that are now rich spawning beds and marine bird colonies.

While the glaciers were melting for the last time, about 10,000 years ago, the land again began to rise, free of the massive weight of ice. Rivers, fed by the melt, raged over the land, carrying tons of mud, sand and gravel. These spillways created the gravel pits south of Caledon. The fascinating spillway at the Mono Cliffs Park occurred as a river flowed between the main escarpment and an outlier, a section of the escarpment that isn't linked visibly to the main body.

Farther north on Highway 89 between Violet Hill and Primrose is evidence of broader development of this watercourse. The Violet Hill spillway, and others associated with it, emptied into the Erie and Huron basins. Similar occurrences are apparent in the Credit Valley, and perhaps at the Humber, which eventually emptied into the Ontario basin.

Finally, as the glaciers disappeared altogether, the ancient lakes retreated, leaving sea caves exposed metres above the waterline. Sand dunes at Huron's shore are evidence of the retreating lakes. Rivers disappeared, replaced by spring-fed brooks.

Five hundred million years were required to create the cuesta. The interminable process of erosion continues as the Earth ages and new formations are born.

With the aid of this book, we hope to walk you along the Giant's Rib. As you walk, do so with the respect due its age.

This is a fragile area, in every aspect as monumental and invaluable as European cathedrals, castles and ruins. Often,

as we worked on this project, we were stunned by the beauty at our own back door, beauty that rivalled anything we'd seen abroad. In this area there are 37 species of orchids, some indigenous to the escarpment alone, as well as ferns, 100 species of trees and 320 species of birds.

We were, however, dismayed by what our fellow human beings had allowed to occur. Private property had been vandalized so that a waterfall could be seen, precious flora had been trampled, and debris left behind. There is something unspeakable about finding a beer can among moss-shrouded roots.

And then there is the problem of developers and reckless loggers. One stand of northern holly fern now lies exposed because a logger did a clear cut rather than a selected cut. In another area, sensitive orchids have been buried by a developer's bulldozer. It's time to ask ourselves, does our need for profit justify such destruction? Or should paradise be locked away, cocooned by protective injunctions so severe that no human being could possibly damage the ecosystem? Or is there a middle way that would permit people to appreciate and not despoil natural wonders?

Perhaps the answers lie in management policies that would balance public access and environmental protection, allowing people to enjoy the land while preserving it for future generations. People need to be restricted to designated paths and boardwalks and instructed through detailed booklets.

While we found this kind of public-minded preservation prominent in the southern regions, to the north, from Mono Cliffs on, there seemed to be little in the way of public awareness, and little government support, though park management work desperately to preserve their areas. With even minimal cooperation among landowners, the Niagara Escarpment Commission and other private and public institutions, boardwalks can be constructed through sensitive areas to keep foot traffic controlled, accurate data published and circulated through tourist and information centres, maintenance established and continued. This is done at Crawford Lake Conservation Area, which contains not only the rare archaeological find of a 500-year-old Huron village, but also a fragile wood with a rare meromictic lake.

The preservation of the Niagara Escarpment is not entirely the responsibility of the Niagara Escarpment Commission. Nor is it the sole responsibility of the different conservation authorities, the Ministry of Natural Resources or Parks Canada. The preservation of the escarpment is the responsibility of every landowner, every visitor, every person who cares to have a heritage to pass on to their children.

It's this kind of commitment that all of us need to make to the Niagara Escarpment. For instance, you need only read the signs along the Bruce Trail to realize their importance: Carry out all litter. Leave only thanks. Take nothing but photographs.

We are rich in natural history. The land is our heritage. And so, as you go, carry out your litter, adhere to designated paths, travel through the land as the native people did—without noise, or mark, or memento.

This book takes you from south to north along the escarpment, and is divided into nine tours corresponding to the nine Niagara Escarpment Commission maps, with a tenth to cover Manitoulin. Geographic and historic wonders are highlighted.

Much of the tour you will be able to drive, along routes that avoid main thoroughfares whenever possible. As we journey farther north, there are areas that can only be travelled in a four-wheel-drive vehicle or on foot, as some of these roads are seasonal or unassumed by the local municipalities. Some roads are just plain steep and rocky. Many areas can only be seen by walking, such as along the Bruce Trail or into parklands.

When you travel on foot, sturdy hiking boots or walking shoes are recommended, as much of the land is only veneered with soil and proves to be slippery. You should be aware, as well, that massasauga rattlesnakes and coyotes are present from Hockley Valley north; also lynx, bobcats and timberwolves are found in the northern regions of the Bruce. The rattlesnakes, by the way, are more afraid of you than you are of them. Please leave them alone.

The northern section has plant species unchanged from the glacial period. Two new national parks exist here—Fathom Five Marine Park (Canada's first national marine park) and Bruce National Park. They are welcome additions to our national commitment to environmental preservation.

To the south is the Carolinian Canada Zone, the warmest region in the country. Here certain plants and animals live in their most northerly extreme, often unique to our land.

If you walk quietly, with care, you will be surprised at the wildlife you will be privileged to see. We have found mink and weasels to be bold, to the point that we've eyeballed one another for several moments. Your heart will flutter to the sound of grouse and partridge drumming—something you feel more than hear—and everywhere there are turkey vultures, incredible scavengers that effortlessly ride the updrafts of the escarpment. White-tailed deer are almost everywhere. You may also see black bears, opossums, badgers, grey foxes, green and great blue herons, beavers, bluebirds, northern mockingbirds...and on and on.

Don't forget about the plants at your feet. Remember those orchids, ferns, seedlings and most especially mosses and fungi. Some mosses and lichens are slow to grow; should they be removed, 20 years of growth can be destroyed, something I discovered, much to my chagrin, after collecting moss for my bonsai collection. Leave the moss alone. The flowers are equally fragile. Zealous photographers have been known to *prune* surrounding flora in order to capture the perfect shot of that rare orchid. Do that, and you may very well destroy the system that supports the rare orchid. Leave the flowers. Leave the fungi. These things belong to the land.

After you read this book and explore the Giant's Rib, we hope you will come to feel as passionately about the escarpment as we do. For now, enjoy.

Map Legend

Protected zone	
Wetlands	
Tour route	
Highway	403
County road	25
Other road	
Seasonal road	

Forest of trillium

THE CAROLINIAN CANADA ZONE

The southern escarpment, areas one to three, is part of Canada's warmest region, the Carolinian Canada Zone. It is unique in that it shelters flora and fauna found nowhere else in the country, as well as a number of endangered species, such as the eastern cougar, West Virginia white butterfly, and cucumber tree. If you consider that the region contains less than one-quarter of one percent of Canada's total land mass, 25 percent of its population, and 50 percent of our endangered species, you'll begin to grasp the fragility of the ecosystem. Of all Ontario's natural areas, this is the most threatened.

Although there are pockets of sanctuary where forests and wildlife are protected, they are threatened by development and pollution directly adjacent to their borders. If ever public awareness and cooperation were needed, it is here—from municipal governments, from developers, from landholders.

Much has been done already. Land stewardship programs under the Carolinian Canada Committee began a few years ago with much success. However, more is needed.

What can you do? Contact the Carolinian Canada Committee, the Federation of Ontario Naturalists (FON), the Niagara Escarpment Commission (NEC), the Ontario Heritage Foundation or any one of numerous organizations committed to preserving our natural and cultural heritage. There are many ways that you as a landowner or a concerned individual can aid in the protection and preservation of this area. Heighten your awareness of environmental contaminants in the products you consume. Recycle. Be a natural gardener. And most of all, consider some kind of cooperative effort with government agencies.

If you own a historically significant building, even if that significance is local, consider putting it under historic designation with the Ontario Heritage Foundation, or contact your Local Architectural Conservancy Advisory Committee (LACAC). A designation doesn't mean you lose rights to your property, but simply that the property will have some measure of protection from development.

Laura Secord Homestead, Queenston

1

Niagara Falls to Grimsby

Much of this southern area was peopled by the Neutral, otherwise known as the Attiwandaron, until the war with the Iroquois in 1650–51. By 1653 there were only 800 known Neutral existing as a separate people. Others took up habitation with friendlier bands of Ojibwa (called Chippewa in some regions) farther to the north on the Bruce Peninsula, or were absorbed into Iroquoian nations. For many years these lands lay relatively uninhabited, until the Mississauga and Chippewa migrated from the Manitoulin area. These were the nations the United Empire Loyalists encountered in their flight from American persecution.

Loyalists first entered the area about 1783, forever changing the face of the land. In 200 short years they and their descendants were to strip the forests, cause the lowering of creeks and pollute the crystalline waters.

Our tour through this area goes from Niagara Falls to Grimsby. The length of the tour depends entirely on you. If you're puddlers like Gary and me, it will take you about seven days. If you prefer the fly-by tour, you can travel the area in just over a day.

For listings of restaurants, accommodations and attractions not included in this tour, we suggest you contact Festival Country Travel Association, listed in the directory called For Further Information at the back of this guide. In that section you will also find contacts for the many conservation authorities, tours and attractions covered in this and subsequent chapters.

Begin at the Niagara Parkway just north of the bridge to Chippewa at King's Bridge Park, a lovely spot to picnic.

Continue north on the Niagara Parkway, across Dufferin Island and into Niagara Falls. For our tour of Niagara Falls, we suggest you walk the length of the falls and then consider the following tours:

The *Maid of the Mist* cruise, 5920 River Road, lasts about 30 minutes. You will pass directly in front of the American Falls, the Rock of Ages and Cave of the Winds, and the Horseshoe Falls. Raincoats are provided and there is bilingual commentary. There is an admission charge and wheelchair access. Contact the office for hours and rates.

To really understand this area, you should also tour Table Rock Scenic Tunnels, through the rock and to a view of the Horseshoe Falls. The address is Table Rock House, Niagara Parkway. There is admission.

An excellent double-decker bus tour, lasting one and a half to six hours, takes you to the Scenic Tunnels, *Maid of the Mist*, Great Gorge Trip, Spanish Aero Car, Niagara Parks greenhouses, Niagara Glen, the School of Horticulture, and to lunch at either Queenston Heights or the Whirlpool Restaurant. Ticket kiosks are located at Table Rock, Victoria Park Restaurant, *Maid of the Mist,* and the Niagara Parks Commission Rapidview parking lot.

And when you tire of geological and cultural history, wander through the Niagara Parks Commission's fabulous gardens. Don't forget the Lundy's Lane Museum.

Niagara Falls

The king of waterfalls enthroned himself here, in the surging water of Niagara Falls. Aboriginal people from all nations made offerings of tobacco to this god, and it was the Mohawks who gave the falls the name Niagara, from Onghiara, meaning "thunder of the waters."

Natives believed the falls originally fell from Queenston Heights. Evidence in the rock strata indicates that the falls originated even farther south than native history suggests, in the vicinity of Lewiston, New York.

Before the Great Lakes as we know them had formed, about 12,000 to 13,000 years ago, there were glacial lakes now referred to as Lake Algonquin and Lake Iroquois, which stretched beyond lakes Erie, Huron, Michigan and Superior. The powerful forces of erosion wore away the escarpment area around Queenston until finally the underlying layers of shale crumbled, releasing the hard cap of dolomite about 10,000 to 11,000 B.C. That was the birth of Niagara Falls.

Old Welland locks, St. Catharines

Daffodils at Niagara Falls

Erosion has continued to grind at the shale, at a rate of 0.3 metres (1 foot) a year, a rate that has slowed considerably from the 1.5 to 1.8 metres (5 to 6 feet) a year before the hydroelectric power generators were installed. In fact, the gorge has taken 35,000 years to reach its current form.

Niagara Falls is considered the world's most powerful waterfall, averaging a volume of about 6,000 cubic metres (212,000 cubic feet) a second. That is to say, a ditch stretching coast to coast would be flooded in one hour.

The appearance of humans near Niagara occurred sometime about 9000 to 7000 B.C., as we know from the discovery of ancient stone tools. At the falls' origin in Lewiston, N.Y., human skeletons from the Mound Builders were found from the period circa A.D. 160. Later, about A.D. 1000, other natives had villages near the falls and river, farming an area until it was no longer supportive and then moving on, allowing the land to regenerate. The river, however, always provided bountiful salmon and sturgeon, until more recent times.

For 14 kilometres (9 miles) from Lewiston to the upper river, above the first rapids, there was an ancient portage, with parts so steep that it was known as Crawl-on-All-Fours.

From the Attiwandaron we first learned of the thunder god Hinu, who lived in the falls. Hinu is the basis for the legend of the Maid of the Mist.

Hinu's wrath was incurred when the Attiwandaron failed to make an annual offering of fruit and game in a canoe sent over the falls. Disease devastated the tribe. Their graves were desecrated and bodies eaten. Seeking to appease Hinu, they sent their most beautiful maiden, along with fruit and game, over the falls in a canoe.

Pestilence and disease continued despite the repeated sacrifice of maidens. Desperate, the tribe sacrificed Lelawalo, the much-loved daughter of Chief Eagle Eye. But her father was determined to go with her, and at the last moment he followed in his own canoe, pitching over the falls too. Eagle Eye died, but Lelawalo was saved by Hinu's sons, who lived in the Cave of the Winds. They told her of the great water snake who lurked on the river bottom, how it poisoned their water and would have to be killed.

Lelawalo returned to her people as a spirit and warned them. When the snake finally appeared from the upper river, the tribe attacked, and though it was not killed outright, it was mortally wounded. Hinu made use of it. Its head was embedded in one side of the rock, its tail in the other, forming a curve that is now the Horseshoe Falls.

The forests surrounding the area were abundant, supporting a wide variety of flora and fauna. The Attiwandaron cultivated 17 varieties of maize, 60 varieties of beans, 8 squashes, and harvested 34 types of wild fruits, 11 nuts, 38 varieties of leaf, stem and bark substances, 12 varieties of edible roots and six fungi. This didn't include the 12 beverages and 11 infusions of parts of plants employed as occasional drinks. Maple sap was their sweetener.

Etienne Brûlé, an outrageous coureur de bois, was the first white to observe the falls, in 1615. Word of Brûlé's experiences encouraged Father Jean de Brébeuf to make his journey inland with conversion in mind. The Attiwandaron had no interest in his religion, but the Hurons did, and Brébeuf began his campaign among them, which eventually led to his death at the hands of invading Iroquois.

Father Hennepin and La Motte were the advance scouts who first reached the falls. Hennepin's description of Niagara Falls, in a volume published in 1683, caused a stir in Europe. Just above the falls, La Salle built the ill-fated *Griffon*, the first ship to sail the Great Lakes. She disappeared on her maiden voyage.

Following the American Revolution, many Loyalists streamed across the border. John Burch, one of Butler's Rangers, a militia unit that had joined the British cause, was among those who settled in the Niagara area. He first harnessed the river to run several mills. His sawmill, situated approximately where the building of the former Electrical Development Company (Toronto Power Plant) now stands, was in proximity to the vast virginal forest to be felled and converted into riches.

The area developed quickly. A tavern was built, then homes, another sawmill and a grist mill. Eventual excavation of one mill led to the discovery of gas, used for lighting.

The War of 1812 stifled burgeoning business. When the enemy retreated from the Battle of Lundy's Lane, they burned Bridgewater—houses, mills and all.

Much of the area was rebuilt after the war, and the economy was largely agrarian, without any real centre. Even as early as 1820, however, tourism to the falls played a major part in the economic well-being of the area.

In 1832 Capt. Ogden Creighton purchased land and named the tract for his home in England—Clifton. The settlement that grew there was renamed Niagara Falls in 1881. The City of Niagara Falls incorporated in 1903.

The tremendous force of water continues to erode all we see. In 1954, Prospect Point, 185,000 tons of rock, rumbled down to the talus at the American Falls. That incident renewed efforts to "save the falls." Two years later, the Schoellkopf Power Plant collapsed in another rockfall, caused when the rock was weakened by honeycombing, or drill holes, during the pioneer era. Surprisingly, only one man died.

Today, the area thrives as both a tourist centre and an industrial centre.

Continue north along the Niagara Parkway out of Niagara Falls—where you will find several historic plaques, parks and tours—and into Queenston. Brock Monument will be visible before you. At the T intersection, turn right. Rather than take a guided tour through the village of Queenston, we suggest you simply walk here and at the heights; almost every street has historic sites. Don't forget to visit the Laura Secord Homestead on Partition Street. The heroine of the War of 1812 overheard American soldiers, who were dining in her home, planning an attack on the British Forces. She walked 30 kilometres (19 miles) to warn the British. Her house has been restored to its 1803 condition and is operated as a museum. There is admission.

Queenston

First known as Queen's Town in the 1780s and named for the Queen's Rangers stationed there, the village was very much affected by development at Newark, now Niagara-on-the-Lake, and later by the re-establishment of the province's capital at York. Queenston was originally significant both militarily and to trade, having a barracks and a docking facility.

One of the important battles of the War of 1812 was fought at Queenston Heights. Under Lieut.-Col. Solomon Van Rensselaer, the Americans were to launch an attack from Lewiston on Queenston Heights. Blinded by his assumption that any attack on the heights would be foolhardy, Maj.-Gen. Isaac Brock and his men remained unaware as a small force crept up a fishing path to the prominence. Brock was forced to retreat, leaving the Americans in control of Queenston Heights.

Long hours of bloody battles ensued, taking the lives of Brock and his next in command, Lieut.-Col. John Macdonell. Only when Maj.-Gen. Roger Hale Sheaffe took command of the demoralized, confused troops did events turn in favour of the British.

Sheaffe directed the Mohawks under his command to attack the Americans' left flank. Sufficiently terrified by this action, the remainder of the American landing force refused to cross, stranding their troops on the heights. All but 30 of the light infantry then circled with Sheaffe to the rear of the heights, surrounding the Americans.

In resulting battle, Americans jumped for their lives from the heights until American Lieut.-Col. Winfield Scott surrendered.

The 64-metre (209-foot) column at the heights is a memorial not only to Brock and Macdonell, but to all those who fell fighting to create the nation of Canada.

If you have a love for theatre and quaint towns, excellent shopping and charming inns, take a side trip to Niagara-on-the-Lake. Because of space we are not including it on our tour but do recommend the town to you.

Head west out of Queenston along York Road, also known as Niagara Regional Road 81, towards St. Davids. Watch for the numerous old stone houses along the way.

Niagara Police Commission Building

St. Davids

Atop Ravine Hill near St. Davids was Stamford Park, the home of Sir Peregrine Maitland, lieutenant-governor of Upper Canada from 1818 to 1828. It was a 22-room mansion, which burned down shortly after 1828. Stone from the foundation forms part of the cairn marking its historic significance, a cairn that also commemorates the largest native ossuary ever uncovered in the province, directly across the highway from the Maitland home. The ossuary was discovered in 1828.

At the crossroads of St. Davids, turn left onto Creek Road, which is Regional Road 100, and right onto Mountain Road, Regional Road 101, where we will travel across the top of the escarpment. Go over the QEW to Beech Road and turn right to Woodend Conservation Area, on the east side.

Woodend Conservation Area

Forty hectares (98 acres) in size, Woodend Conservation Area offers hiking, cross-country skiing, year-round day use, as well as interpretive and educational programs. Picnic tables are available. There are also historic buildings from the former homesteaders—a lime kiln, a gazebo and the foundations of the original home. Bruce Trail enthusiasts should note that the trail goes through the area. There is no admission.

Go back to Beech Road and continue north to the lights at Regional Road 89. Turn left to cross the Welland Canal bridge and turn right at Canal Road. Several places afford an opportunity to view the locks.

Welland Canal

The idea of a canal to bypass Niagara Falls and cut through the escarpment challenged entrepreneurs and settlers for a long time. As early as 1699, Vauban, a French engineer, proposed the idea. Another French engineer, De la Mathe, reworked the plan and presented it to court in 1710. Both times the proposal fell on deaf ears.

In 1793, Robert Hamilton, a Queenston merchant, made a proposal to Governor Simcoe. Simcoe didn't act on it either, for fear it would create a monopoly for its owners. A few years later, the Americans entertained the same thought with the same results. Nothing.

It wasn't until 1824, under William Hamilton Merritt, that enough government support was garnered to bring the project to realization. Funding came from everywhere after Merritt blitzed the countryside to raise money. There were to be 40 wooden locks, each 33.5 metres (110 feet) long by 6.7 metres (22 feet) wide in the

chamber, with a depth of water 2.4 metres (8 feet). The cost of each lock was to be £550.

Construction was hazardous and working conditions poor, housing inadequate, and wages low for the predominantly Irish labourers. Fever and malaria were common.

The escarpment is an area riddled with springs and notorious for poor drainage on the gently sloping edge of the cuesta. Near Port Robinson, a powerful well was hit, carrying one workman to his death. That underground water necessitated a change in plans.

Engineers intended to divert water from elsewhere, but quicksand at the other source imperilled equipment. The plan was again changed; water would instead be diverted from the Grand River, which was at a higher level.

All these problems caused incredible financial burdens to the Welland Canal Company. Public opinion turned against the builders. The drinking water became unfit, and the company, instead of supplying its labourers with fresh water, equipped water boys with whiskey.

Needless to say, the opening of the wooden Welland was delayed. Despite setbacks, the Welland did open in 1829, five years after construction first began, effectively circumnavigating Niagara Falls. As a result of the canal, not only was trade by water made easy, but mills sprang up in abundance—32 by 1847.

Since then, there have been many alterations, additions and much upgrading, and the original course has been abandoned. Unlike the first Welland, the new Welland links lakes Ontario and Erie.

Today, the canal is still considered one of the marvels of engineering, joining the Great Lakes and the North American continent with the St. Lawrence Seaway's passage to the Atlantic through eight locks. Ships are lifted 99.5 metres (326 feet) between Lake Ontario and Lake Erie.

At Lakeshore Road, turn left to cut across the lower end of St. Catharines. On the northeast corner of Lakeshore and Canal streets, you will notice a cantilever bridge.

St. Catharines

St. Catharines probably owes its origins to the building of a native bridge across Twelve Mile Creek. In fact, the main street of St. Catharines, St. Paul Street, is the site of an ancient trail, as are Queenston, Niagara and Merritt streets, and Martindale and Pelham roads.

When the French came in search of furs and commerce, they did little to displace aboriginal people. The British were responsible for the massive settlement that was to follow and, sadly, for the displacement of the natives.

Settlement in the St. Catharines area took place before the land was actually surveyed, and the town as an entity didn't emerge until the turn of the nineteenth century, when it was little more than an inn at the crossroads. Servicing settlers gave St. Catharines its foundation, as it was to become the local centre for agricultural equipment, seed grain and livestock, and general domestic supplies. Customers made yearly visits, then monthly ones as roads were improved.

By 1792, St. Catharines was established as an Anglican mission settlement. Growth ensued, with taverns, storehouses, mills, schools, smithies, and the beginning of a potash and timber exchange.

With the War of 1812, development in the village halted, though it, unlike many villages of that time, was not burned as the Americans retreated.

Merritt acted as a catalyst to further development of the village after his release as a prisoner of war from the Battle of Lundy's Lane. He set up a dry goods store, a hardware and grocery store, ran a grist mill and developed a saltworks at a salt spring. To produce one bushel of salt, 757 litres (200 gallons) of water had to be boiled. He went on to own a potashery, a distillery and a blacksmith's shop.

Perhaps the most significant change for St. Catharines occurred when the Welland Canal cut through the escarpment and ran along the town's border. Water was then in adequate supply and was often diverted for mill races. As well, Irish immigrants came by the hundreds for the guaranteed employment the canal offered, and that in turn boosted the economy. Trade that flowed through the waterway enhanced the successes St. Catharines had already known.

The saltworks owned by Merritt was later purchased by Dr. William Chace, who had been Merritt's partner, when Merritt became involved in the Welland Canal. That sale sparked the beginning of St. Catharines as a spa resort.

Chace had observed that the pigs Merritt kept, and watered from the saline spring, were unusually healthy. Under his ownership the salt spring became a bathing establishment. Increasingly familiar with the beneficial effects of the water, Chace began in 1847 to bottle it from his 150-metre-deep (490-foot) artesian well. The following year his plans were curtailed when fire destroyed the saltworks.

Under Col. Eleazer Williams Stephenson, the works was turned into a hotel business, known as St. Catharines House, after he purchased the burned-out saltworks and had a sample of the water sent to a chemistry professor at the University of Toronto. The results of the test revealed that the spring water contained chlorides, iodides, bromides of calcium and magnesium, and sulphates comparable to the curative waters of famous European spas. In 1853, he built an even larger hotel, which was to be known as Stephenson House, at Yates and Salina streets.

Spas sprang up everywhere. In the same year, another hotel, Welland House, was built on the corner of King and Ontario streets, and by 1856 St. Catharines was well known as a resort town.

It's not surprising that the mineral springs were so popular. This was the Victorian Era, when the affluent gorged on 12-course meals and suffered from acute constipation. Drinking the water (rich in Epsom salts) provided relief to patrons who came from as far away as the American South.

Dr. Theophilus Mack, aware of the water's laxative property, began bottling water from a sulphur spring in 1856. Mack opened a sanitorium in 1864. It later became Springbank, one of the town's preeminent resorts.

Interest in spas declined from the 1860s—during the American Civil War, which bankrupted many Southern landowners. In 1888, Springbank was sold to Bishop Ridley College and destroyed by fire in 1903.

Stephenson House was purchased by Demill Ladies College in 1898. Ridley College took over the premises in 1903. Sometime in 1916, after Ridley College moved to its new buildings, Puccini Macaroni Factory began production in the old spa, where pasta was churned out until 1930, when fire destroyed the factory. The shell of the building was demolished the following year.

The last survivor, Welland House, evolved into the Welland House Hotel. The springs still surface in the basement, but they are now regarded as a nuisance and pumped into the sewers to prevent flooding.

Today, the Garden City area produces half of the province's fresh fruit.

Continue along Lakeshore, which runs into Ontario Street after the lights. You will now be travelling in a southerly direction, hugging Twelve Mile Creek. At Glenridge Avenue, turn right, and then right again at Glendale, which becomes Pelham Road after the lights. Off to your left, keep an eye out for the hydro spillway. Turn left at DeCew Road to visit DeCew Falls.

DeCew Falls

DeCew Falls was named for John DeCow. DeCow purchased 40 hectares (100 acres), including the falls, from a native for an axe and a blanket, and an additional 40 hectares for a gold doubloon. The term *purchase* is perhaps an inappropriate term, for the natives still "owned" the land, inasmuch as they ever thought of themselves owning land, but allowed DeCow to live there.

Here he built a sawmill and oil mill. The oil mill was the first of its kind between Lake Erie and Lake Ontario and was an instant success because of the importance of flax in those early days. Originally, flax was grown solely to be turned into linens. The rich oil-bearing seeds were too costly to process and until the advent of DeCow's oil mill were often left unused.

The mills, however, were at the mercy of the streams, which often dried up during the summer months and were torrential during flood seasons. The dry season became

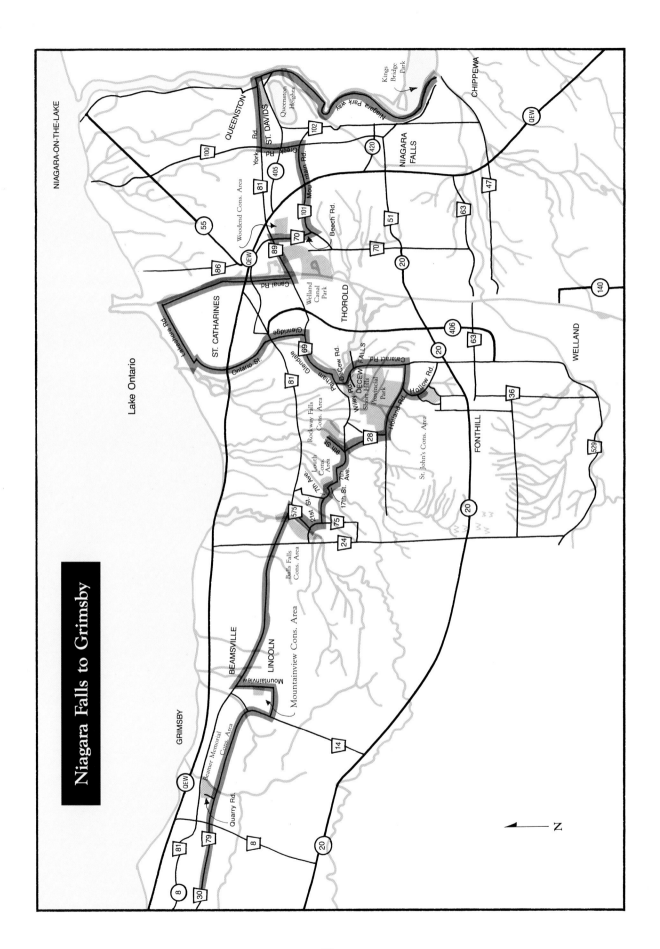

Niagara Falls to Grimsby

DeCew Falls, St. Catharines

more and more extended, to the point that the mills eventually had to be closed.

On DeCew Road, you will find to the left the old Morningstar Mill and Mountain Hills Museum. The mill was built in 1872 as a flour and grist mill, suffered fire in 1895, was rebuilt, and remained in continuous use until 1933. The property is owned by Ontario Hydro, which repaired the mill and leased it to the City of St. Catharines. Admission is free, and there are picnic areas and parking.

Continue along DeCew Road and turn right at Cataract Road. At Wiley Road, turn right and follow it to the end, to a parking area for the Short Hills Provincial Park.

Short Hills Provincial Park

Short Hills Provincial Park is 645 hectares (1,594 acres) in size and is under the auspices of the Ministry of Natural Resources, and one of the escarpment's nodal parks. Short Hills has also been recognized as a Carolinian Canada Zone reserve.

The land drained by Twelve Mile Creek—so named because it is 12 miles west of the Niagara River—is known as the Short Hills. The valley is about 3.2 kilometres (2 miles) wide and 6 to 8 kilometres (4 to 5 miles) long, in places 91 metres (300 feet) below the tableland and 68 metres (225 feet) above. It was formed during the last ice age and was part of the Lake Ontario depression, then known as Lake Iroquois, and filled with ice 91 to 121 metres (300 to 400 feet) above the tableland. The Attiwandaron used the area as their wintering grounds.

Go back along Wiley Road to Cataract Road and turn right. Continue south to Holland Road and turn right, and then left at Hollow Road, into St. John's Valley. Hollow Road is yet another that follows a native trail.

St. John's Conservation Area

St. John's Conservation Area covers 32 hectares (79 acres) and includes a portion of the only cold-water spring-fed creek in the Niagara Region, Twelve Mile Creek. There is a man-made trout pond where you may fish. You may also hike along the trails, which are especially lovely in spring and summer because of their flowers.

There is an outdoor studies centre here, established in 1970 by the Niagara South Board of Education. It's open 10 months of the year, offering courses to students from kindergarten to Grade 13. Other programs are located in the Upper Canada Schoolhouse, built about 1804, also owned by the Board of Education.

Because the area is sensitive—the steep slopes of the hills are largely sand and susceptible to erosion—the Niagara Peninsula Conservation Authority has restricted development of the park.

A unique aspect of the area is the forest, one of the few remaining Carolinian forest regions in Canada. The rare (for Canada) species found here include the sassafras, tulip tree and black walnut.

It's sad to think that, prior to the eighteenth century, everything to the horizon was part of this cathedral of green that now remains only in sheltered, isolated pockets. St. John's Conservation Area continues to be a sanctuary for many endangered species. However, this sanctuary may not remain capable of sustaining those endangered species, considering the pollutants from surrounding development.

The village of St. John's thrived in the early 1800s. It was a manufacturing and service centre settled by Benjamin Canby in 1790. With his brother-in-law John Darling, Canby built a sawmill, grist mill, brickyard, fulling mill, tannery, potashery, woollen mill and iron foundry. Merritt's mills farther downstream, along with the Welland Canal, destroyed development in St. John's.

Go back along Hollow Road and turn left onto Holland Road. At Regional Road 28, turn right and take the gravel road farther along at the forks towards Rockway Falls. Directly ahead at the intersection of Regional Roads 28 and 69 is a small area where you can pull over for an excellent view of the falls.

To get to Rockway Falls Conservation Area, continue west along Regional Road 69 to 9th Street and turn right.

Rockway Falls Conservation Area

The Rockway Falls Conservation Area is classified as a nature reserve. Its 85 hectares (210 acres) are used primarily for picnicking and hiking. The falls themselves are 40 metres (131 feet) high.

Part of the Carolinian Canada Zone, the area has examples of sassafras and flowering dogwood. Natives used the split stems of the flowering dogwood for toothbrushes.

One of the earliest salt wells ever sunk in Upper Canada exists here, and there is a ruin of a lime kiln.

Drive back along 9th Street to Regional Road 69 and turn right. At 7th Avenue, turn right towards Louth Conservation Area.

Louth Conservation Area

The area is a 32-hectare (79-acre) nature reserve in the escarpment plan and is great for hiking, nature appreciation and viewing. A small parking area is available.

Turn right out of the conservation area on 7th Avenue to 17th Street. Turn right at 17th, and then left where 7th Avenue continues. At 21st Street, also known as Regional Road 75, turn right and follow the conservation signs into Balls Falls Conservation Area.

Balls Falls Conservation Area

Camping, hiking and day activities are possible on this 90-hectare (222-acre) property. There are two falls—2 kilometres (1.2 miles) apart. Rock strata are plainly visible along the gorge: at the upper falls, the caprock of grey-brown dolomite is known as the Lockport Formation; beneath this is the greyer stratum of DeCew dolomite, then the dark grey shale, blockish in appearance, of the Rochester Formation.

Farther downstream, below the lower falls, lies exposed Irondequoit limestone, then Reynales Formation dolomite, which is characterized by dark grey shale partings. The green-grey layer of sandstone and shale indicates part of the Thorold Formation, under which is a red stratum of the Grimsby Formation and the banded silt and shale of the Power Glen Formation.

To understand what the original forests were like, visit the section known as the Bert Miller Arboretum. Species reintroduced here include two types of mountain ash, flowering dogwood, ironwood, balsam, Canada and Allegheny serviceberries, and red maple.

Still in existence are the flour and grist mill of 1809, log cabins, the lime kiln, a blacksmith shop, an apple-drying shed and an 1864 church. There is paid admission to the conservation area. Picnic areas, washrooms, food concessions, barn and church rentals are available.

Just a bit of trivia: this is the second sunniest location in Ontario.

Bahl, now known as Ball, had enterprises with his brother here at the falls. The area became known as Glen Elgin after some of Butler's Rangers sold the land to the Balls in 1807. A grist mill built in 1810 was operated by George Ball, a miller. The dam was situated above the falls to ensure an even flow of water, and the mill was run by a 9-metre (32-foot) overshot wheel that turned four sets of grindstones, with the wheelhouse carved out of the limestone rock.

By 1840, the water level of the creek was falling, so the mill was converted to steam power. In 1890, the western end of the mill was removed, including two sets of grinding stones.

Flour was packed in barrels and bags and shipped out through Jordan Harbour or hauled by team to St. Catharines and even shipped overseas to Britain.

In 1827, a five-storey woollen mill operated on the west bank of the Twenty, half a mile from the grist mill. Such enterprises attracted workers, who soon populated both sides of the creek.

The Balls added a water-powered sawmill, which had a cooper's shop where barrels were made for flour. At the lower falls was a smithy. Three lime kilns processed hundreds of tons of lime for mortar. The flourishing businesses passed into the hands of George's son.

The railway ended the area's prosperity. The Great Western came in east below the cuesta, and in 1855 the last ship docked at Jordan. Without shipping facilities, the mills fell into decline. By Confederation, the woollen mill had ceased operation. In 1875, only six people were on the assessment roll. Both the sawmill and woollen mill were dismantled in 1883, and the grist mill served only the neighbourhood trade, despite upgrading to steam in 1896.

Balls continued to live in the community until 1962, when Manley Ball sold the remaining property to the Niagara Peninsula Conservation Authority, ending the family's 150-year tenure.

Follow the road back out of the conservation area and turn left onto Regional Road 575. Turn left at Regional Road 81. Here we'll travel across what is commonly known as The Bench, an area that was once the beach of Lake Iroquois. Continue through Beamsville and Lincoln and turn left onto Mountainview Road to enter Mountainview Conservation Area.

Mountainview Conservation Area

This 25-hectare (61-acre) natural environment park is excellent for hiking.

Head south along Mountainview Road and follow it around the bend to the stop sign at Regional Road 14. Turn right, and keep to the left at the forks, still on Regional Road 14, through the next stop where Regional Road 14 becomes Regional Road 79. At the corner of Regional Roads 79 and 12 is a conservation area marker and stop sign. Follow the marker to the left on Regional Road 12 and then right where Regional Road 79 continues. At the bend is a small area where you can pull over for a good view of Beamer's Falls, following the Bruce Trail markers. To enter Beamer Memorial Conservation Area, continue along Regional Road 79 to Quarry Road and turn right.

Beamer Memorial Conservation Area

The 50-hectare (123-acre) park is an escarpment natural environment park owned and operated by the Niagara Peninsula Conservation Authority. This is a good place for hiking and picnicking, as well as enjoying the spectacular view from Beamer Lookout over the Niagara fruit belt. This is also one of the best places in Canada to chart the migratory route of hawks.

Tews Falls

2

Winona to Lake Medad

To the Chippewa (or Ojibwa), the area from Winona to Lake Medad was a place of manitous, the spirits in every rock, every tree, every body of water. Manitous were evident in the explosions that regularly shook the prominences, something sceptics attributed to sulphurous gas explosions. However, when whites settled the areas of Hamilton Mountain and Burlington Heights, the manitous are said to have fled out of abhorrence for the new race. The explosions stopped.

The area from Winona to Lake Medad is also in the Carolinian Canada Zone, with a few pockets of land under Niagara Escarpment Plan and/or Carolinian Canada Committee protection. There is a great deal to see and do. We will emphasize conservation areas over urban centres, leaving the cultural touring up to you on side trips. This section could take anywhere from two days to a week to see, depending on your pace and choice of activity.

We will continue our tour on Regional Road 79, where we left off at Beamer Memorial Conservation Area. Turn right onto Fifty Road, which descends through protected lands to Highway 8. Turn left at Highway 8 and continue into Winona.

Winona

Winonah was the wife of Epingishimook, an Ojibwa spirit who gave birth to Mudjeekawis, Pepekawis, Chichiabos and the more renowned trickster, Nanabush. Winonah was a soft, beautiful woman, and her name means "soft and beautiful."

Archaeological finds indicate that the area was long inhabited by native people. White settlement occurred about the same period as in the rest of the Niagara Peninsula; however, it wasn't until John W. Wilson built a wharf

Sulphur Springs

that Winona became an important port, servicing the grain industry. When the railway came through, the port declined, then became completely obsolete when the Welland Canal was opened.

Today, Winona retains some of its lovely old homes, which can be seen as you travel through on Highway 8.

At McNelly Road, head left, where the road again climbs the escarpment. To your right will be Vinemount Conservation Area, which has a spectacular lookout. Parking is limited.

Return to McNelly Road, continuing south until you come to Ridge Road, then turn right. This is a lovely drive, with several excellent views of Hamilton. At the forks, keep to the left for Devil's Punch Bowl Conservation Area.

Devil's Punch Bowl Conservation Area

Fed by Stoney Creek, the fabulous waterfall here has formed an enormous bowl, probably one of the more pronounced bowl formations on the escarpment. The sedimentary formations clearly visible here are of interest to geologists.

There are good trails for hikers, no admission, and parking is available.

From Devil's Punch Bowl Conservation Area, continue along Ridge Road to Highway 20 and turn right. Again we will descend the escarpment, into Hamilton. At Centennial Parkway, turn right for the Stoney Creek Battlefield Park.

Stoney Creek Battlefield Park

One of the important battles of the War of 1812 was fought here. On a sultry June night, under the cover of clouds, events were to coalesce around James Gage's house. The American army had advanced, taken the family captive in the cellar and set up a field office.

In the meantime, the Canadians were preparing at Gage's uncle's farm some little distance across the road on another hill. It was between these two homes that the Battle of Stoney Creek took place. Guides at the park can provide details of the battle.

Perhaps the best time to visit is during the re-enactment of the battle, held annually on the first weekend in June. For more information, contact the Hamilton Region Conservation Authority listed in the back of this guide.

Head back to Centennial Parkway and Highway 20, climbing the escarpment again, travelling south until you reach Mud Street, which is also Regional Road 11, and turn right. At Paramount Drive, make another right and continue to Ackland. At the crescent of the street is parking for Felker's Falls Conservation Area.

Felker's Falls Conservation Area

A mill, situated halfway down the gorge on a flat shelf of rock, was built there in 1795 by William David. Its foundations and wheelpit are still visible.

A trail is accessible to wheelchairs. Tapes are available for the vision impaired.

Continue around the crescent of Ackland, which will take you back to Paramount Drive. Return along Paramount Drive to Mud Street, make a right and head to King Forest Park, which is also Mount Albion Conservation Area.

Mount Albion Conservation Area

The village of Albion Mills boasted three sawmills and a grist mill, but after 1880 they were no longer profitable and the village disappeared. A sister community, Mount Albion, remained, having three hotels, two blacksmiths, a general store and several taverns.

Opposite the falls is a perpendicular wall of rock 30 metres (100 feet) high, called Lover's Leap. An early inhabitant, Jane Riley, disenchanted with her lover, Joseph Rousseau, threw herself from the precipice and died.

Look south towards the hill and you will see where Cook's castle once stood. Built about 1840 by William Cook, it was a five-storey stone structure with 14 fireplaces on 161 hectares (400 acres) of virgin forest. After Cook's death in 1870, fire destroyed the many large barns; the castle was pulled down and the estate lost to the family.

Head north along Mountain Brow Boulevard. This is a tricky road to follow, with spectacular views, so stay alert.

At the first circle, keep bearing to the right, heading downward, and continue right along the partial cloverleaf, and back up the escarpment to Sherman Access. Please note that the cloverleaf exit to Sherman Access is closed from 9:00 a.m. to 6:00 p.m. Monday to Friday. Continue on Sherman Access at the lights at Sherman Cut. At the next circle, stay on the westbound access, which will take you to James Street and then to Mountain Access Road West. If you can peel your eyes away from navigating, note the many beautiful old homes along this section.

Make a right at the first lights on Mountain Access Road West, which takes you to Fennell Avenue West. Make a left at Garth Street, a right on Denlow Avenue and another left on Scenic Drive (which it is, by the way). At Mohawk, turn right. You will travel over the 403. At Highway 2, otherwise known as Wilson Street, turn right towards Tiffany Falls Conservation Area. You're now on the edge of Dundas.

Hamilton

This sprawling metropolis was founded by George Hamilton, who moved here one year after the War of 1812, to take up residence on farmland he'd purchased with the intent of surveying and division into town lots. Like so many town founders, he named the streets after his children—John, James, Catharine, Hannah, Maria and Augusta.

The city is located on a narrow plain 2.4 to 4.8 kilometres (1½ to 3 miles) wide, between the escarpment to the south and the bay and adjoining marsh to the north.

When the area was inhabited by aboriginal people it was primarily a swamp fed by streams that flowed from the foot of the escarpment. Deep inlets were lined with meadows and clay hills that supported scrub pine, oak, maple, ash, hemlock, spruce, walnut, beech, chestnut, butternut and hickory. Along the waterline grew willow and elm, providing an ideal sanctuary for waterfowl. Saw-toothed Indian swordgrass bound the soil and provided homes for mosquitoes, dragonflies, mayflies, craneflies and myriad other insects; these and fishes, crustaceans and plankton supplied ample food for the birds.

Mammals were also in abundance—bears, deer, wolves. Bears and wolves were the white settlers' enemies, and as more land was settled, the natural habitat for indigenous species declined, placing enormous pressures on the predators to find other prey. Calves, sheep, chickens, even small children became that prey.

The sludgy brown waters of Hamilton Harbour were once touted as the finest natural harbour on the Great Lakes and called *marcassah*, meaning "beautiful waters," by the native people.

The waterways of the St. Lawrence and the Hudson-Mohawk systems were to play an important role in the way Hamilton grew, as were a surplus of groundwater and a lack of rapid streams. Hamilton developed slowly as a mercantile base, rather than experiencing the sudden development that had occurred around so many mill sites. As an agricultural region, however, it boomed.

Settlers swarmed to the area faster than surveyors could lay it out, and some even squatted on land before negotiations between the Mississauga and British took place. As they had in most of the southern regions, Loyalists were to dominate early settlement from the late 1700s onward. The first recorded settler in the Hamilton area was John Depue (later Depew), Sr., and his brother-in-law, George Stuart, who arrived about 1783.

Depew's claim is now the 375 hectares (935 acres) where much of Hamilton's present industry stands: the Steel Company of Canada Limited, Canadian Industries Limited and many others.

To the west of the Depews and Stewarts, Robert Land struggled on property beyond a long finger of Lake Geneva (now Burlington Bay).

The three families were joined about 1785 by Richard Beasley, who came to set up a trading post with the Mississauga to the west on Lake Geneva. He constructed a wharf and storehouse on the beach.

By 1791, his entrepreneurial interests had expanded from fur trading to milling. He built a saw- and grist mill in what was to later become Ancaster. Beasley was not an astute businessman, however, and left himself nearly indigent.

In 1816, George Hamilton, the son of wealthy magnate Robert Hamilton, established the town of Hamilton. He purchased the most important piece of real estate below the mountain in the present city of Hamilton. The family settled in a stone mansion known as Bellevue. Through a series of chance circumstances, he was able to sell land to the Crown for the building of a courthouse and jail, market-place and promenade. This left him wealthy. Some of the remainder of his land he subdivided. The land sold slowly, and it was in this fashion that Hamilton grew.

If you love gardening, visit the Royal Botanical Gardens. For information about the RBG, refer to the section For Further Information at the back of this guide.

On the south side of Wilson Street look for Tiffany Falls Conservation Area, which has a waterfall and hiking trails. Parking is available.

Go back along Wilson Street to Sulphur Springs Road, a lovely twisting road with many vistas.

Continue on Sulphur Springs Road as it turns to the right. If you travel directly ahead, you'll be on Mineral Springs Road and off our tour. Once you find the road to the right, you'll come to one of the entrances to the Dundas Valley Conservation Area.

Dundas Valley Conservation Area

To the left of the road is the sulphur spring, which has been tapped, and around which has been erected a monument—all very pretty but providing no idea of the spring's natural form. Stop here to inspect this odorous wonder or hike along the trails.

This is a valley typical of the escarpment. It was created by a pre-glacial river, the Erigan, which cut through from the west, beneath the ice, and emptied into Lake Iroquois along a sandbar in Hamilton beneath York Street. As the Wisconsin ice sheet retreated, the flow of the Erigan lessened to the point that the mighty river is now no more than a creek. The valley it carved, however, remains.

Here in Dundas Valley, the upper part of the gorge was filled with sand, gravel and boulders as the sheet melted. Even now there is evidence of the ancient riverbed; well diggers find limestone in one area but not to either side.

Hamilton Harbour, visible from the hills around Dundas

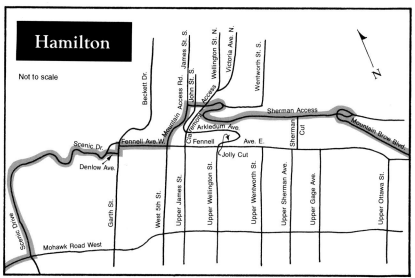

Hamilton

Not to scale

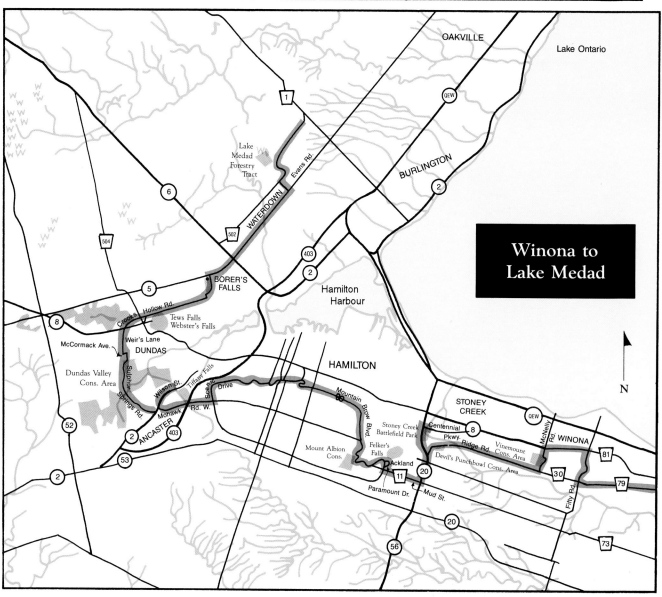

Winona to Lake Medad

British troops at the re-enactment of the Battle of Stoney Creek

American troops at the re-enactment of the Battle of Stoney Creek

Valley, was formed after the glacial retreat. Lake Iroquois ended in a triangular bay much like Hamilton Harbour but farther inland, where the town of Dundas now sits. As the Wisconsin sheet retreated and freed the upper St. Lawrence, the level of Lake Iroquois dropped and the harbour receded to form the present-day body.

The Dundas Valley had been used by the Attiwandaron as a trail to circumnavigate the escarpment.

Surprisingly, the first white settlement in Dundas Valley was established by a woman, Anne Morden, a Loyalist who fled her home in America in 1787 after her husband had been unjustly executed. When the British gave land grants to those loyal to the Crown, the Mordens received holdings for almost all the northern half of what is now the town of Dundas, as well as into Flamborough Mountain.

In 1789, Morden's family was joined by the Showerses, who settled on the Ancaster side of the valley on 242 hectares (600 acres) around Webster's Falls.

The area was to remain primarily rural until the turn of the nineteenth century, when the first grist mill came into existence.

This area has now been identified as part of the Carolinian Canada Zone.

Continue along Sulphur Springs Road. Turn left at McCormack Avenue, right at Weir's lane, right again at the T intersection. At Crooks Hollow Road, turn left. Around the bend are the ruins of the Darnley grist mill, built in 1813 by James Crooks. A little farther along is the Crooks Hollow Conservation Area. We invite you to visit, but have not included it in our tour.

Continue along Crooks Hollow Road to Short Road. Turn right, and then right again at Fallsview Drive. Here you'll find the entrance to Webster's Falls. The falls themselves are marvellous. There is talk, however, of a hydro project going in here, which would be unfortunate.

To get to Tews Falls, simply backtrack along Fallsview Drive, turn right at Short Road, right at Crooks Hollow Road and continue along for a few hundred metres. Parking is available to the right.

From Tews Falls, continue along Crooks Hollow Road, which becomes Harvest Road. You will round a bend to the left. At this corner is a historical plaque marking the site of the old Rock Chapel. Another bend to the right leads you to Borer's Falls. There is no parking, so pull well off the road and use the trail.

Go back to the car and follow Harvest Road to Highway 5 through Waterdown.

Waterdown

Grindstone Creek runs through the village of Waterdown, rushing over a cataract and on to the south. Here an Attiwandaron trail led to Lake Medad, and white settlers established mills and forged a community.

The first inhabitant, Alexander McDonnell, was a Loyalist who arrived in the vicinity about 1796. He left his lands undeveloped. Because he also had the mill rights, and had failed to develop his property, the grant fell to Alexander Brown in 1805. Brown established the first mill at Great Falls. The mill was purchased in 1823 by Ebenezer Culver Griffin, and under Griffin, Waterdown really developed into a settlement.

He established a sawmill, a flour mill and a woollen mill. His son, James Kent Griffin, built a toll road from Hamilton to Carlisle in 1853, now known both as Snake Road and Centre Road, which follows the ancient Attiwandaron trail.

Like most early towns, Waterdown expanded its services to meet the needs of increasing numbers of settlers, so that by 1867 there were 100 householders and 600 inhabitants.

At the four corners of Waterdown is The American House, an inn probably built about 1841. On the corner opposite is Weeks' Hardware, dating from the turn of the century. To the other side of the road is a lovely stone building, once a bank. The village's oldest homes can be seen if you take a side trip down Griffin Street.

Continue along Highway 5 to Evans Road and turn left. Make a right at the T intersection, to Parkside Drive. Continue along Parkside Drive, which is also No. 1 Sideroad. The forestry tract is inaccessible to the public, but the lake, leased by a golf course, can be visited.

Lake Medad Forestry Tract

Near Lake Medad, named for farmer Medad Parsons, was an Attiwandaron village known as Kandoucho, discovered about 1640 by Jesuit missionaries. The Jesuits were barred from the village and returned to the more receptive Hurons.

Kandoucho was located on a rocky ledge along Lake Medad's eastern shore. Above it is an ossuary.

The lake, leased by the Medad Heights Golf Course, actually forms part of the Niagara Escarpment Commission's protected zone. It is 6 metres (20 feet) deep with a surface area of 16 hectares (40 acres). Bottom ooze extends for 18 metres (60 feet) above the bedrock.

Although the lake is fed by several creeks, there is no known outlet. Despite this, it remains at a relatively stable level. Geologists believe an underground source feeds it directly into Lake Ontario.

3

Mount Nemo to Silver Creek

Our third tour, through an area of cliffs and canyons, marks the transition from the Carolinian Canada Zone to the Great Lakes–St. Lawrence Forest region. The transition is completed in the next part of our tour. Although gravel-pit activity is extensive, much of the land here—which holds 800-year-old trees, an ancient native village and the remains of Pleistocene waterfalls—is protected under the Niagara Escarpment Plan.

Two days should be adequate for this tour, though if you linger at the Ontario Agricultural Museum and a few of the other attractions you might need three or four days for the trip.

Continue on No. 1 Sideroad near Lake Medad. At Cedar Springs Road, turn left, then right at No. 2 Sideroad. To your left will be a large gravel pit, part of the rich depositions left during the last glacial retreat. Continue through into the village of Mount Nemo, round the bend. At the stop sign, turn right. Just a little ahead and to the left is a sign for Colling Road. To the right is the entrance to Mount Nemo Conservation Area.

Mount Nemo Conservation Area

Mount Nemo is an outlier of the Niagara Escarpment, and an excellent place for rock climbing and spelunking. This natural environment park covers 98 hectares (242 acres). An abandoned quarry lies here but is strictly off limits.

To get to the trails and cliffs requires a 15-minute hike. According to some climbers, the work is well worth the effort, as the limestone cliffs afford superb alpine activity.

There is no designated parking and no admission.

Take the route along Colling Road directly in front of the entrance to Mount Nemo. At Cedar Springs Road, turn right, to wind along the Medad Valley. You'll come to a T intersection in the village of Kilbride. At the T, turn right onto Kilbride Street.

Kilbride

The village was laid out by Francis Baker and William Panton about 1850. The two set up a milling and lumbering business, taking advantage of the surrounding vast forests to supply their sawmill. By 1870, Kilbride was quite prosperous, with a population of several hundred and lots of employment. A general store, a woollen mill, a harness shop, a tailor and churches were evidence of a thriving community.

Follow Kilbride Street to the intersection of County Road 7 and turn left. Go through the stop at Derry Road and continue north. As you enter a series of turns you'll see a sign, none too prominent, to the left, indicating Yaremko-Ridley Park.

Yaremko-Ridley Park

A small lake and green, green forest are the attractions at Yaremko-Ridley Park, 70 hectares (172 acres) of natural environment. About 1915 marl (fine-grained calcium carbonate) was mined here as a filler for insecticide. The ruins of one kiln and a drying rack remain. There is no admission and no parking.

If you care to hike farther north on the road, the Bruce Trail enters Crawford Forestry Tract to the east.

Crawford Forestry Tract

A natural environment area of 123 hectares (303 acres), Crawford Forestry Tract has a dormant waterfall which has been dry for 12,000 years but which was once part of a tributary from Crawford Lake. There is no admission and no parking.

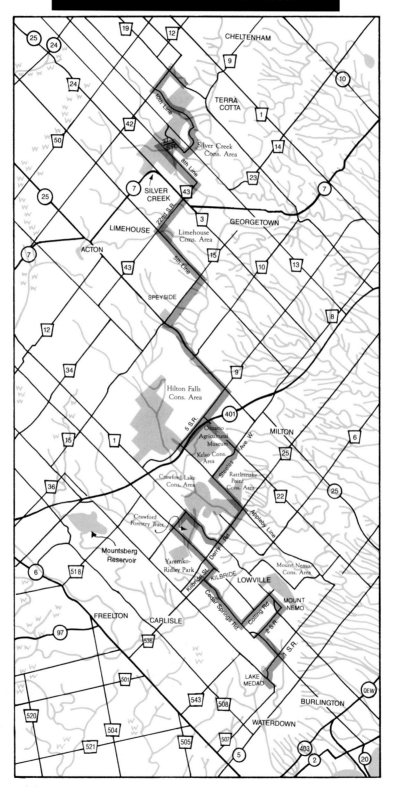

Cedars

Continue north on County Road 7 to Steeles Avenue West, and turn right. At the next intersection continue through into Crawford Lake Conservation Area.

Crawford Lake Conservation Area

This outstanding conservation area contains a 500-year-old reconstructed native village and meromictic lake within a fragile wood. The lake is one of only two of its type in Ontario, Found Lake in Algonquin Park being the other.

A meromictic lake is deeper than its surface area. The upper half of its water mixes hardly at all with the bottom half, and can be described as one body atop another. Because the lower portion is thus deprived of oxygen, it is a scientist's paradise: decomposition occurs at a dramatically slowed rate, so a scientist is able to read the layers of sediment to determine what type of vegetation existed during particular years and what kind of human activity occurred nearby.

Crawford Lake is 24 metres (74 feet) deep. Scientists were able to determine that Crawford Lake is about 15,000 years old, a creation of the retreating glaciers. Groundwater ate away at the soft limestone of the escarpment, creating a solution cave, which results from the slow inner erosion of rock by running or dripping water. When the cave reached a considerable size and was no longer capable of supporting the overhead arch, the roof collapsed, forming a sink- or karst hole, and voilà (in the slow glacial sense), one meromictic lake!

Through discoveries in the lake, archaeologists were able to determine that a Huron village existed here about 1430. Serious investigation began along the knoll to the northeast, uncovering post moulds for several longhouses.

There were nine known longhouses, although only a few have been reconstructed. Such a village would have housed approximately 450 people.

Further investigation revealed that within the vicinity of 5 to 12 kilometres (3 to 7 miles), there had been nine villages, five of them Attiwandaron settlements at the outermost edge, and four Huron closest to Crawford Lake.

Murray Crawford was a pioneer who purchased the tract to provide wood for his steam sawmill, which he operated at the southern end of the lake. So enchanting was the area that he later used it as a retreat for himself and his family. In 1969, the land was sold to the Halton Region Conservation Authority.

There is admission to the village, and picnic areas are available. No swimming is allowed in the lake.

Don't forget about the native festivals—Green Corn Season, Midwinter Season, Thanks to the Maple Season and Spring Season. Such opportunities to walk into the past are rare. Phone numbers are listed in the section For Further Information at the back of this guide.

Leave Crawford Lake Conservation Area and turn left onto County Road 1. At Derry Road, turn left. Just past Walker's Line you will see the entrance to Rattlesnake Buffalo Compound. Details about the area are included under Rattlesnake Point. Continue east to Appleby Line and turn left. The fabulous twisting road heads up to Rattlesnake Point, marked on the left.

Rattlesnake Point

Diverse and spectacular, the 230-hectare (570-acre) Rattlesnake Point Conservation Area is sure to capture your interest. Abutting Crawford Lake Conservation Area and visible for miles, Rattlesnake Point is an area as delicate as it is beautiful. This is also a natural environment park.

Evidence indicates that Rattlesnake Point was an encampment during the Paleo-Indian period of 9000 to 5000 B.C. and was at one time covered by stands of massive white pine. The pines have all but vanished, logged in the settlement rush of the 1800s. Agriculture proved poor in the thin soils of the escarpment, so land was abandoned for more fertile tracts. The existing hardwoods developed later.

There are three important geological features here: the Milton Outlier (of which Rattlesnake Point is a part), the

escarpment and the Nassagaweya Canyon, which was a spillway during the last ice age.

Turkey vultures abound, as do many rare species of flora and fauna. A buffalo herd is maintained. Rattlesnakes, shot in obscene numbers by settlers, are no longer found.

Excellent trails are available for hiking and cross-country skiing. There are areas for picnicking and, for stouter hearts, rock climbing. Many crevice caves have formed, making this location a favourite for spelunkers. The principal cave is a multi-level one leading to a small chamber approximately 15 metres (49 feet) below ground.

Caution should be exercised when walking near the escarpment edge. The drop is precipitous.

There is admission and plenty of parking.

Drive back to Appleby Line, heading north. At Steeles Avenue West, turn right. At the curve of the road is an excellent view of Milton. Should you wish to do some shopping or find a restaurant, we suggest you continue on into Milton. Otherwise, turn left at Townline. To the north, on the left, is Kelso Conservation Area, and a little farther north is the Ontario Agricultural Museum.

Kelso Conservation Area

Kelso is a great place to swim, boat, fish, hike, golf and picnic over 235 hectares (580 acres) of Niagara Escarpment Plan recreational parkland. Glen Eden Ski Area is situated here, and the Kelso Cliffs offer alpine enthusiasts a good climb. The Halton Region Museum, a collection of six buildings built from 1806 to the post–Second World War era, offers a variety of regional artifacts. There is admission. Parking and washrooms are available.

Ontario Agricultural Museum

Designated through the Niagara Escarpment Plan as a historical park, the Ontario Agricultural Museum encompasses 32 hectares (79 acres) of history and nostalgia. The 30 reconstructed buildings are staffed by knowledgeable characters sure to enchant. Perhaps one of the most delightful times to visit is during the steam festival, when the area hoots and churns to the rhythms of old-time machines.

There is admission. Parking, a snack bar and washrooms are available.

Continue north on Townline, across the 401 to the intersection at No. 5 Sideroad. Turn left and head for Hilton Falls Conservation Area, marked on the right.

Hilton Falls Conservation Area

A natural environment park of 952 hectares (2,352 acres), the area was originally settled by Henry Young about 1830.

Bald eagle

Later Edward Hilton built and operated a sawmill at the base of the falls.

The mill's style has been described as odd: its bulkhead was made by scooping out a tree in the shape of a trough. Set on its end into the gorge, it carried water down about 12 metres (40 feet) to a flutter wheel.

When the Louis Riel Rebellion broke out, Hilton abandoned the mill to join in. Vacant for 20 years, the mill fell to ruin. It was restored by George Parks about 1850. This attempt failed too, and six years later the property was mortgaged.

A man named Preiker was the next to try his hand at this ill-fated enterprise, but fire destroyed it.

The conservation area exists to maintain significant headwater control areas of the Sixteen Mile Creek and to preserve the large wildlife habitat and green zone. You can enjoy the extensive trail network, a spectacular escarpment outcrop, beaver meadows and a 14-hectare (34-acre) water reservoir for flood-control purposes, not for swimming because the area is far too sensitive environmentally.

Parking is available. There are day-use facilities only. Admission is charged.

Return along No. 5 Sideroad to the lights at Highway 25. Turn left at Highway 25 and head north to Speyside. At Regional Road 5, turn right. Once you reach Halton Hills 5th Line, turn left and head north to Limehouse. There is an interesting rock cut just before Limehouse.

Limehouse and Limehouse Conservation Area

The village of Limehouse was known as Fountain Green prior to the opening of the post office in 1857.

Because the escarpment is largely limestone, it was mined ruthlessly during the latter part of the previous century and into the beginning of this century. Limestone was essentially useless until heated to temperatures in excess of 398°C (750°F), ground into powder and mixed with water for mortar. The procedure is as old as civilization, having been used in ancient Egyptian, Babylonian and Greek times.

Around the village of Limehouse, the limestone industry sprang up. Early kilns were no more than hollows in the escarpment. Time and demand created more efficient kilns, so that by 1850 Limehouse had five of the squat structures, often built in vertical series. One series could burn 20 cords of wood over three to four days, processing about 800 bushels of rock.

Technology changed the kilns to structures with 1.8-metre (6-foot) walls, which rose above 15 metres (50 feet). A perimeter of 5.4 to 6 metres (18 to 20 feet) was common at the base. Rock would be dumped into the top, because often the kilns were level with quarries, and wood was fed from the bottom. These kilns were far more efficient. One of the hazardous by-products was carbon dioxide, dispersed by giant water-powered fans inside the kilns.

By the early twentieth century, Limehouse had 10 kilns in constant operation, but the boom could not last. The local forest had been devastated and production costs soared. Competition from larger modern kilns closed many of the small operations.

By 1918, Limehouse as a source of lime was no more. The excavation of the escarpment continues, however, in designated areas over which the Ministry of Natural Resources has jurisdiction. We can only hope that preservation will remain important when demands for sand, gravel and other products soar.

Excellent hiking and cross-country skiing are available throughout the 77 hectares (190 acres) of the conservation area.

Turn right off the 5th Line onto 22nd Sideroad and head east, past the stop sign to the 8th Line of Halton. Turn left. This road is not maintained in winter, so you should restrict your travel to other times of the year. The way is steep. Four-wheel-drive vehicles are strongly recommended to make the worthwhile climb up the escarpment.

Near the top, Silver Creek cascades right beside the road, shaded by forest. At the top of the hill, turn right and then right again onto 27 Sideroad. At the corner of 27 Sideroad and Fallbrook Trail is the Silver Creek Valley Conservation Education Centre.

Silver Creek Conservation Area

A Niagara Escarpment nature reserve, Silver Creek encompasses 486 hectares (120 acres). There is no admission, and no facilities are available. To use the nature trail, follow the Bruce Trail markings.

Mono Cliffs Provincial Park woods

GREAT LAKES FOREST

Actually known as the Great Lakes–St. Lawrence Forest, this area continues the transition from Carolinian Forest to Great Lakes Forest. The region extends up to Manitoulin, where another transition occurs, from Great Lakes Forest to Boreal Forest.

Trees in the Great Lakes region are maple, birch, beech and oak, with pine, hemlock, cedar and other evergreens. To our knowledge, there is no virgin forest left in the southern reaches of the zone. All you see is second growth or the result of reforestation.

When European settlement began in this area, the trees were considered obstructions to be cleared in order to improve the land. Although much of the wood did go into the manufacture of fencing and housing, most of the forest was simply cleared and burned.

It's hard to imagine there were once pines 3.6 metres (12 feet) in circumference and 50 metres (170 feet) high, or that the natives built canoes from the birches growing all through this region—freight canoes that could hold tons of goods. (In 1957, Matt Bernard, a Chippewa expert

in canoe-making, had to travel extensively and exhaustively in the Algonquin and Temagami regions to find birch trees large enough to complete his commission.)

Once the land of the escarpment forest was cleared for agriculture, the soil often proved thin and susceptible to erosion. Without tree roots to bind the soil, it simply washed away. Then, as more and more mills used the streams of the escarpment, that pressure, coupled with the denuding of the land, led to falling water levels, so the mills had to cease operation.

For some reason, small pockets of forest were left intact along the escarpment, so there are still cedars estimated to be 800 years old. These are now carefully protected.

As the forests were cleared, wildlife habitat was destroyed. Bears have gone forever. The massasauga rattlesnakes exist, only farther north. Deer, however, found a haven, and now, as more and more people become conservation-minded, coyotes and even wolves are making a reappearance in rural areas.

Spring freshet in Hockley Valley

4

Terra Cotta to Violet Hill

This area is crossed by several rivers, one of which, the Credit, had as many as 45 mills along its length. Being the highest area in Ontario, it is also a watershed where rivers drain to four lakes—Huron, Simcoe, Erie and Ontario.

Here, as in so many regions, gold fever struck during the mid-nineteenth century. Legend suggests that an old native frequented a Scottish family, often displaying gold nuggets. In gratitude to the family for their many kindnesses, he promised to take their son to his secret place. The mother, alarmed that her son should go alone, had the father follow the two men, trailing them to an underground passage. The trek failed there. The native disappeared between two rocks, and the secret of the gold was gone.

That legend prompted a gold rush along the Credit about 1837. Forty percent of prospectors died before ever reaching the Credit Valley. The people in the mining camp contracted scurvy. No gold was ever found.

Rail fever replaced gold fever. Two railways once steamed through the Credit Valley—the Credit Valley Railway and the Toronto, Grey Bruce, the latter a narrow-gauge line.

To construct a railway through this rugged country was no easy task. It required a climb to the top of the escarpment of 117 metres (385 feet) in 9 kilometres (6 miles).

Touring this section will probably take three to four days, allowing time to explore the many conservation areas.

At the 27th Sideroad of Halton Hills, turn right at Fallbrook Trail and follow it as it meanders to Clayhill Road. Turn left at Clayhill Road, and left again at Halton 10th Line. Follow the 10th Line to the Erin Halton Townline and turn right. At Winston Churchill Boulevard, turn right again. This will take you to the Terra Cotta Conservation Area.

Terra Cotta Conservation Area

The conservation area was established as a Niagara Escarpment natural area and operates under the auspices of the Credit Valley Conservation Authority. Consisting of 160 hectares (395 acres), with multi-use recreational facilities, it is one of the 10 nodal parks along the escarpment.

The red Queenston shale dating from 400 million years ago is evident along many riverbeds. Here, in the conservation area, the Credit River finds one of its sources in groundwater that flows into five man-made ponds in the day-use area, and from the spring-fed northerly ponds of Muskrat Pond and Wolf Lake.

At one time there were black bears, lynxes, fishers, wolverines and elk in the area, but as settlement occurred and habitat was destroyed, the large mammals were driven out. Before mill effluent, there were northern salmon in the Credit River.

About 1550, a Huron village was located 4 kilometres (2.4 miles) northeast of the conservation area.

Today, if you're quiet and careful, you may see deer, mink or great blue heron.

Fishing, hiking, swimming, camping, cross-country skiing and picnicking are all activities to be enjoyed here. There is admission, parking and an interpretive centre.

Follow Winston Churchill Boulevard to the south and into the village of Terra Cotta.

Terra Cotta

Henry Tucker, a settler, built a grist mill in the area in 1855 and later a sawmill. These enterprises led to the development of the village, which was first called Tucker's Mill. Janet Plewes and her son, Simon, subsequently took over the mills, and the settlement became known as Plewes' Mills. The family also began a brickworks, which made use of the local red clay.

By 1866, the village was named Salmonville, because of the bountiful salmon in the Credit River, and boasted a hotel, inn, general store, post office and Methodist church. Still the village grew, stimulated by the Hamilton Northwestern Railway. A forge and carriage shop, telegraph office and another grist mill were added.

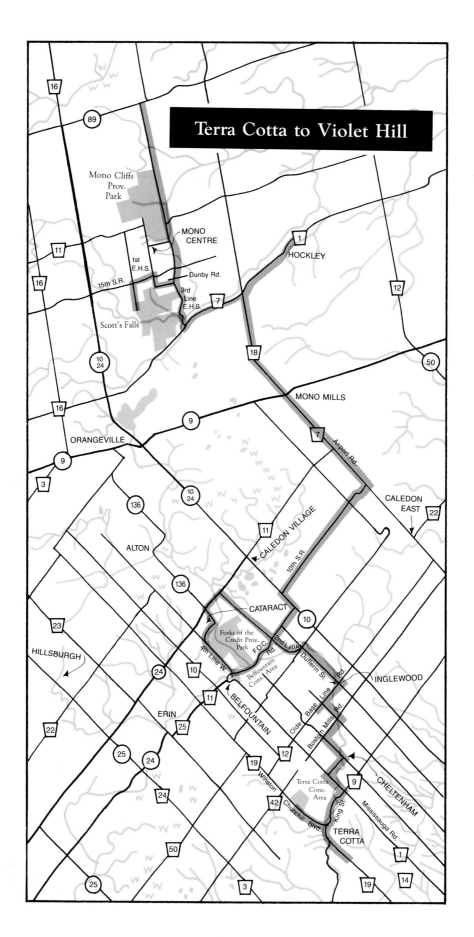

Terra Cotta to Violet Hill

However, by the time the village became known as Terra Cotta (meaning baked earth), a decline had set in; the soil had been depleted of nutrients by overfarming and many businesses had closed. After a series of rejuvenations and declines, the Great Depression hit the village, closing the brickworks. Terra Cotta subsided into a quaint tourist area.

There is a legend of a ghost at the Plewes' mill. It seems the night-watchman at the mill often saw a white apparition drift through, so he stalked the spirit with a double-barrelled shotgun. On cue, the spirit appeared from under the mill wheel. When the watchman accosted the spirit, however, it was no ghost but a flesh-and-blood man who wanted to buy the mill and thought he might get a better price if it were haunted.

There are many delightful shops and restaurants in the village.

After you've exhausted yourself browsing and eating, continue east on King Street. As you reach the summit of the escarpment, the old brickworks will come into view. At Mississauga Road, turn right and then right again on Mill Street into the village of Cheltenham.

Cheltenham

Unlike most settlement towns, Cheltenham didn't develop according to a regular grid plan because of certain natural obstacles: the Credit River flowed through and the Niagara Escarpment rose steeply from the valley. So Cheltenham just sort of grew, a little here, a little there, sprawling in an easy way.

Charles Haines, a millwright, arrived about 1820. By 1827, his grist mill was in operation as the principal business, until 1945, when it burned down.

The first years of Cheltenham, from 1827 to 1850, were ones of growth and excitement. From 1850 to 1890, Cheltenham enjoyed its prosperity, bolstered by the railways and small shops. But the village could not survive the mass production of the twentieth century, so it became a lovely, sleepy town for a weekend visit.

Head north out of Cheltenham to Boston Mills Road and turn right into Boston Mills.

Boston Mills

Named for an old song, "The Road to Boston," Boston Mills was established by two young Welshmen, David Williams, and his brother John, about 1821. The old Boston Mills cemetery dates back to 1823, when David was killed by a tree he was felling.

Other settlers came, cleared the land and raised families. By 1833, a schoolhouse was erected. The village had a distillery, a tailor, who later became the postmaster, and an organ maker.

The mills of Boston Mills weren't built until about 1850, probably by Hiram Caslor. His was a sawmill. Prosperity gave Caslor the freedom to open a carding mill. In 1860, a grist mill was erected, but not without problems. Caslor, it seems, underestimated building costs and required an additional $200. Such a sum might as well have been a million in those days. However, Mrs. Caslor, a thrifty woman, gave her despondent husband a stocking filled with sixpence and shillings, and financed the added cost of the mill.

The mills subsequently changed hands several times. So prosperous did the village become that it even had a grain elevator along the Hamilton & Northwestern Railway, and a hotel to service Boston Mills' visitors.

Inglewood, to the north, was outpacing Boston Mills and became a major centre owing to the junction of the two railways. As a result, Boston Mills declined. The flour mills were razed and in 1884 the hotel was closed. About the same time, the grain elevator was destroyed and little was left of the village.

The dam remained and was used by Shale Products Limited, which installed a dynamo to generate electricity for their Inglewood plant. The establishment later became the Cataract Light and Power Company. In 1931, the dam was washed out in flood season.

Today, there is little left of Boston Mills.

Turn left on Chinguacousy Road, left on Olde Base Line Road. About 1 kilometre (0.6 mile) west, on the south side, is a series of fascinating terra cotta moguls. Park well off the road to prevent accidents and to view the moguls from a distance (foot traffic damages the formation, and the owners may resent trespassers).

Turn around, head east on Olde Base Line Road to Dufferin Street and turn left to the village of Inglewood.

Inglewood

This town developed over a period of 20 years, probably beginning with the Loyalists in the 1830s. In 1843, Thomas Corbett built a dam and woollen mill, and the town burgeoned.

Continue north out of Inglewood on Dufferin Street. There is an interesting view here of the Credit Valley. At the 5th Sideroad, turn left. Veer to the right at the 2nd Line and cross a lovely little one-lane bridge. After this you'll be able to see Devil's Pulpit behind you. At the Forks of the Credit Road (Peel Regional Road 11), turn left.

Terra cotta moguls

Devil's Pulpit

A high wall of dolomite, Devil's Pulpit caused much speculation among settlers until the natives explained how it came to be.

A young man, who camped with his band on the edge of an escarpment cliff, loved a woman from a nation to the south. Her family, not fond of the man, denied her to him in marriage. Not to be put off, he, with a group of men, raided the neighbouring camp and seized the maiden, taking her to his camp. A battle ensued, during which her clansmen were driven off. But the woman wasn't happy with her husband. She fretted and died. The thunderbirds in retribution created a violent lightning storm, sundering the young man's camp from the land and leaving him marooned. There he died.

This was not to be the end of the thunderbirds' wrath: both tribes were punished when all game and fish disappeared from the area. No trace of the people remained.

Continue along the Forks of the Credit Road to the Forks of the Credit Provincial Park.

Forks of the Credit Provincial Park

Outstanding historic and natural features mark this escarpment natural environment park of 282 hectares (696 acres). There is hope that the MNR will be able to procure an additional 65 hectares (160 acres) for the purposes of erosion control and environmental protection.

The lakes within the park are kettle lakes formed by the last glaciation. As well, a portion of the old Dominion Road runs through the area.

There is no admission, sparse parking, and excellent picnic areas are tucked in among the trees. The trails are extensive and well worth a day of hiking. Fishing is allowed: there are excellent stocks of brook and brown trout. We'll explore the Credit River and leave the waterfall and powerhouse ruins for our visit to Cataract.

Return to the Forks of the Credit Road and turn right, heading for Belfountain Conservation Area, which is posted on the left just before the village of Belfountain.

Belfountain Conservation Area

In 1908, Charles W. Mack, a wealthy manufacturer of rubber stamps, purchased a strip of land by the Credit River for his retreat. Originally he erected a cottage called Lucke-nuf for himself and his family, and later a 12-person guest house known as Bide-a-wee.

During his tenure, the lands were cleared. The stone fountain and bell on the property soon came to symbolize the village of Belfountain. A mini Niagara Falls with swing-ing bridge, several picnic and swimming areas and lookouts were added.

Carl Uteck purchased the property in 1946, turning it into a tourism business venture. William Gress Rogers, the next owner, developed the land further for its tourism value and ran an establishment until 1959. At that time, the Credit Valley Conservation Authority acquired the land, continuing to add property until 1973. The cottages and buildings were demolished and facilities improved.

Covering 12 hectares (29 acres), Belfountain Conservation Area offers swimming, fishing, nature trails, picnic areas and washrooms. There is admission.

Continue west on Forks of the Credit Road into the village of Belfountain.

Belfountain

Like so many frontier villages, Belfountain grew around water—in this case the Credit—and owing to the efforts of a determined man—here, "Grize" McCurdy. Although the first settler was William Frank, who built a dam and grist mill on the West Credit River, McCurdy for many years dominated the settlement known, inevitably, as McCurdy's Village.

While the gold rush of the Credit Valley attracted many men, McCurdy was seized by silver fever. He had a silver mine east of Belfountain and west of the Forks of the Credit, near Devil's Pulpit. Later a group of miners began a shaft for a silver mine in a depression known as Hogg's Hollow.

That McCurdy or the other miners actually found silver seems unlikely, as silver, like gold, isn't found in sedimentary rock. These men probably found minute quantities of lead, which has a silvery appearance when first cut.

Between Forks of the Credit Road and Mill Street (River Road), near the grist mill, is the location of McCurdy's sawmill. He had agreed to rent it to a Quaker named Bull, but the transaction ended in disaster. The two argued about rent, and McCurdy, in a fit of temper, hit Quaker Bull. The Quaker retaliated with a blow from an implement, sending McCurdy sprawling. In the fall he hit his head on a stone and died.

The village eventually grew to include several quarries, mills and a tannery—enterprises of a healthy industrial centre.

The general store on the corner of Main and Busch streets was originally the site of the Glover Tavern. McCurdy, opposed to drinking establishments, refused to sell land to Glover. Despite this, Glover purchased the land on the corner and built the tavern. When it was complete, William MacDonald of the village climbed the rafters, broke a bottle of whiskey over the beams and proclaimed:

Fountain and flower garden, Belfountain Conservation Area

And so this building, it did rise,
Independent of Old Grize.
The old miser wouldn't sell,
So let him go plumb to hell.

A cooper named McNaughton was responsible for Mc-Curdy's Village being called Tubtown. To advertise his business making tubs, he erected a 12-foot-diameter tub-like building, much to the chagrin of neighbours. When McNaughton left for Erin, the sobriquet Tubtown persisted.

The name Belfountain came into existence sometime between 1852 and 1857, appearing on maps as Bellefountain. Over the years the spelling was altered to Belfountain.

Backtrack along the Forks of the Credit to the east for about half a kilometre (one-third of a mile). Take the 4th Line West, to the left. There is a Forks of the Credit Provincial Park sign here. This is a lovely, winding drive up the escarpment. Turn right at Cataract Road, and about 300 metres (320 yards) on, to the right, is a private road with two buildings. This is a natural spring owned by Canada Dry and known as McLaughlin Spring.

McLaughlin Spring

Back in 1910, J. J. McLaughlin knew the Credit Hills were filled with springs, and being an enterprising man, he purchased 40 hectares (100 acres) on both sides of the CPR tracks, on the west bank of the West Credit River. There he established White Mountain Spring Water under the company name McLaughlin-Hygea Waters, bottled the water and sold it. Later, this company became known as Canada Dry; its first soft drink was Canada Dry Ginger Ale.

Although the Credit Valley division was closed in 1920, trucks are periodically to be seen at the spring, filling with fresh water for both Canada Dry and Crystal Springs Water.

Continue along Cataract Road into the village of Cataract. We suggest you find a convenient place to park, roam the village and then take the walking tour described below.

Cataract

While searching for gold, William Grant came upon a salt spring frequented by deer. Excited by the discovery and the prospect of a business there, he convinced his employer in

44

York to underwrite an expedition. The village of Gleniffer sprang up, complete with a sawmill and shacks. The salt, however, eluded Grant, as it was buried too deep within the hills to extract, and the village was abandoned.

In 1858, Richard Church purchased Gleniffer for $100 and renamed it Church's Falls. When the railway came through, the people of the village renamed it Cataract to avoid confusion with Churchville to the south. In the village's heyday, there were saw-, grist and woollen mills, a stave and barrel plant, a broom factory and a brewery, which closed in 1865.

The Horseshoe Inn, now Cataract Inn, was built in 1855. It is one of the few remaining buildings from the village's early days.

The church on William Street was built about 1890. Now a private home, it has been designated a historic site. We ask that you respect the owners' privacy.

Walk to the Forks of the Credit Provincial Park entrance and hike down the trail, which will take you to the cataract also known as Church's Falls.

Church's Falls

If you look beneath the falls to the hollow behind, you'll see the area that was quarried for stone for the sawmill later belonging to the Wheeler Brothers, settlers who came to the area in the early 1800s. In 1890, John Deagle purchased the burned-out Wheeler Brothers mill for $1,800 and used it for a time as a grist mill.

A clever man who invented the spinning-tub washing machine, he realized competition would devour his meagre profits and in 1892 converted the mill to a power plant. He was successful, coming on line at Cataract in 1899. Ten years later, Erin was one of his customers. The business expanded so that by 1928 his system supplied Hillsburgh, Forks of the Credit, Brimstone, Belfountain, Caledon Village, Inglewood, Cheltenham, Caledon East and the townships of Caledon and Chinguacousy.

He eventually sold to Ontario Hydro, which closed the operation in 1946 and dynamited the buildings in 1953. Cataract Lake is now gone, leaving only hulking cement walls and ruins.

Hike back to the village, to your car, and travel along the 3rd Line (which runs into Cataract Road), north through what was Coulterville at Highway 24, and turn right. Continue east along Highway 24 to the 2nd Line West. Turn right. At the Forks of the Credit Road, turn left and continue to Highway 10. Head north along Highway 10 to Caledon Sideroad 10, and turn right. On a clear day, there are some magnificent views of Toronto from this height. Follow Sideroad 10 to Airport Road. Turn left at Airport Road and head north into the village of Mono Mills.

Mono Mills

The establishment of this town, about 1820, can be attributed to Michael McLaughlin, the builder of the first sawmill. A grocery and drygoods store and an inn were built later. In 1853, William Campbell ran a tannery. Mono Mills grew until it had five hotels, five blacksmiths and a carriage works.

The name Mono is derived either from the Ojibwa word meaning "let it be" or from Gaelic *monadh,* meaning "hill."

When the railway bypassed Mono Mills, the town declined, but recently subdivisions have been built, and because the area is close to Toronto, it has become one of the city's bedroom communities.

Continue along Airport Road, cross Highway 9 and make the spectacular descent into Hockley Valley. This is one of the most breathtaking drives in Ontario, though during a winter blow it can be hair-raising. At the bottom of the valley you will come to a set of warning lights at the intersection of Airport and Hockley roads. Turn right onto Hockley Road and head for the village of Hockley.

Hockley

Named for Thomas Hockley, a settler who spent no more than two years here, the village of Hockley still endures. Of interest is the location of The Driveshed, a general store operating in the same building as the general store and post office of 1837. The village at one time also had a hotel, sawmill, shoemaker, blacksmith and veterinarian. Located on an ancient native trail that wound from Mono Mills to Mono Centre, Hockley is now a quaint tourist area with interesting shops, a tearoom and a steakhouse.

Head back along Hockley Road towards the 3rd Line E.H.S. (a local designation meaning East of Hurontario Street) Mono Township. As you travel, take note of Woodside Lodge to the north, just past the 5th Line. Built in the 1930s, it was one of the earliest tourist centres in the valley, attracting more than 2,000 visitors in its first full year of operation.

At the corner of the 4th Line and Hockley Road was the village of Glen Cross. Just east of the 3rd Line, on the north side, is a white stucco house that at one time was the Glen Cross Inn, probably built in the 1930s. Just beyond our turn to the north at the 3rd is Glen Cross Pottery, where the original Glen Cross post office was situated.

Go north along the 3rd Line. The way is steep and winding, and if you decide to hike or drive slowly, the view behind is lovely. Deer often cross here at dusk. Continue to Dunby Road and turn west towards the 2nd Line E.H.S. and then head north. At the 15th Sideroad, turn west

Mono Cliffs Provincial Park

Wild turkeys

again, then south to the 1st Line E.H.S. Drive till you run out of road and come to a private road. We're headed for our favourite waterfall, Scott's Falls, or, as some know it, Cannings Falls. From here we hike along the Bruce Trail. You'll have to work for this one!

Scott's Falls

This sensitive area, which includes a series of three cataracts, is full of mosses, ferns and orchids. Curb your wanderlust, though, as much has already been destroyed by careless hikers, illegal campers and revellers. On the Ministry of Natural Resources' lands abutting the falls, severe damage has been caused by trailbikers. Please note that here you'll be travelling on the private property that the Bruce Trail runs through.

Much of the strata of the escarpment lie exposed at the falls, a joy for geologists. Bluebirds nest here, as a result of the commitment of landowners to the preservation of their natural surroundings. The area is suspected to have been once used by native people as a summer village. It is known that the manitou of the falls was revered.

Hike back to the car and return the way you came, back to the 3rd Line E.H.S., and head north. Turn left at the first intersection. To the north, just before the village of Mono Centre, is the southern entrance to Mono Cliffs Provincial Park.

Mono Cliffs Provincial Park

Designated a low recreational use natural environment park, Mono Cliffs is a fabulous place to spend a day or an afternoon. There are crevice caves here, a spooky outlier forested in cedars that weave a dense carpet of roots over hidden caves, and much in the way of wildlife and flora. This hike is one of our personal favourites. However, we do ask you to adhere to the designated trails, as the area is sensitive. There is no admission and some parking is available.

Go back to the car and head west along the 18th Sideroad into the village of Mono Centre.

Mono Centre

This is the oldest village in Mono Township and is now the township seat. Mono Centre was never to develop beyond a service centre for local settlers, owing to the lack of sufficient water power or mineral deposits. The Mono Cliffs Inn was formerly the general store and post office.

Backtrack east and continue around the bend of the paved road. Turn left at the 3rd Line E.H.S. where it continues to the north and Violet Hill. Settled by William Bowers about 1830, Violet Hill remains a sleepy village. It was named for the hill to the northeast, which was at one time carpeted in violets.

Hart's tongue fern

5

Boyne Valley to Nottawasaga Lookout

North of Highway 89, the escarpment becomes a paradise of valleys. With infinite slowness the Boyne, Pine, Noisy, Mad and Pretty rivers carved the sedimentary and dolostone rock, creating fertile valleys that lured and defeated the early settlers. Such adventurous people were drawn by the promise of farmlands, breathtaking scenery and the hope for a better life. Towns sprang up in this vast rural land, particularly when Hurontario Street (which now often follows Highway 10) blazed northward, and for a time the settlements flourished.

As other centres grew, and easily accessible roads linked them, the settlements along the escarpment, more particularly along Hurontario Street, withered. It was easier to ship goods, particularly lumber from the vast stands of pine, to Shelburne, Creemore, Stayner and Collingwood. Towns and villages such as Glen Huron and Dunedin remain much as they were in the late 1800s. Others, such as Ruskview, Whitfield and Lavender, virtually vanished, except for their churches, cemeteries and schoolhouses.

The valleys and rivers are just as lovely as when the Hurons and later the Chippewa passed through.

Some of the areas in this section are on private land, so please respect privacy. As always, we ask you to move with care among the delicate flora.

The tour itself should take no more than two days, though if you choose to forgo some of the hikes, you can drive through the area in one.

Head west from Violet Hill on Highway 89 to Primrose, and then north on Mulmur Township Line 1 W.H.S. to Boyne Valley Provincial Park. Circle the park around to the east at the 5th Sideroad and enter the park via the Bruce Trail at the foot of Concession 1 E.H.S.

Boyne Valley Provincial Park

Although it's a provincial park, Boyne Valley is classified a natural environment area, encompassing part of the Violet Hill spillway, and is known as the best example of a spillway in Southern Ontario. The park covers 434 hectares (107 acres). No plans have been made to develop it beyond its use by cross-country skiers and hikers. The Bruce Trail runs through the area. An outdoor education centre here is owned by the Toronto Board of Education.

The bottom of the Boyne Valley is very swampy. We suggest you dress accordingly.

Backtrack along the Bruce Trail to your car and continue north on Concession 1 E.H.S. to the old Primrose cemetery on the left. The village of Primrose is back at the intersection of highways 10 and 89, its cemetery at the 5th and 1st concessions roads.

Continue north on Concession 1 E.H.S. to Dufferin County Road 17 to the hamlet of Whitfield, originally known as Whitley Settlement. Its church is all that remains.

Head west along 10th Sideroad Mulmur to Highway 24 and turn right. Take the Hornings Mills cutoff.

Hornings Mills

In 1830, Lewis Horning and three other men slashed their way northward to Pine River, determined to make a settlement. They found a place bordered on the north by a rich hardwood forest, on the south by a series of small lakes that became sites for their grist and sawmills, on the west by vast beaver meadows, cedar swamp and swales, and by the Pine River Valley on the east. This became Hornings Mills.

All did not go well for Horning. A cow in calf had taken to a nearby swamp, and Lewis Horning, Jr., and children from the Van Meer family overheard Horning, Sr., saying to one of this hired hands that he would pay a dollar to have the animals fetched. The children, determined to earn the money, set off and were never found, despite an extensive search.

Townsfolk accused the natives of kidnapping the children. Even 20 years later, when a young man turned up claiming to be Oliver Van Meer, nothing concrete was discovered. He told a story so full of contradictions that he

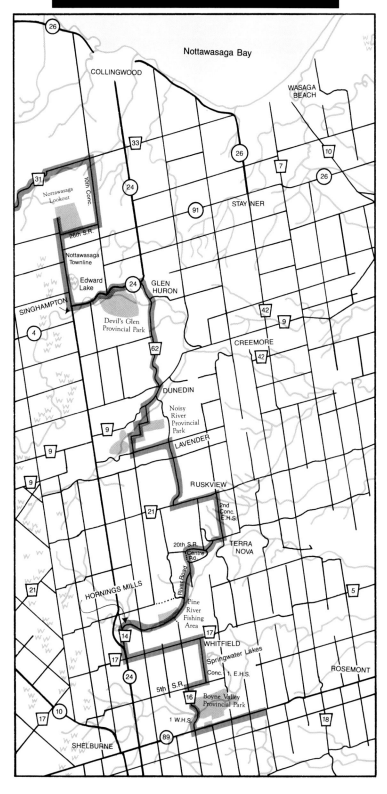

Coyote

was not believed. Distraught, Horning sold his businesses to William Airth in 1838 and left town.

There is much of interest here in Hornings Mills, a place worth a leisurely visit.

Head east out of Hornings Mills along River Road to the Pine River Fishing Area; the first entrance is to the left.

Pine River Fishing Area

Encompassing 80 hectares (197 acres), this area is managed by the Ministry of Natural Resources for fishing. Rainbow trout are stocked from April to May. Fish ladders farther along were created to provide a route for migrating fish from Georgian Bay up the Pine River, after the MNR built a dam to create the 4-hectare (10-acre) pond.

At one time the land was owned by the Dufferin Light and Power Company. An enormous dam spanned the river, over 30 metres (100 feet) high, generating power into the early 1900s.

When Ontario Hydro came into existence, many of the smaller companies suffered, and Dufferin Light and Power Company closed its doors. Hurricane Hazel in 1956 destroyed the dam and many of the buildings. Ruins can still be seen on the trails.

Continue east along River Road. A second entrance to the Pine River Fishing Area is to the left, with ample parking and outhouses. A little farther east along River Road are the fish ladders, also on the left. This area is worth a visit and has a small parking area. Otherwise, continue east on River Road into the village of Kilgorie, marked now by only its school, built in 1909.

Following River Road to the east, take Centre Road and climb the hill for a spectacular lookout across the Pine River Valley. Part of this road is seasonal, and if you can, continue through to the 20th Sideroad Mulmur. Turn left at the 1st Concession East towards Terra Nova, or head back down to River Road and follow it into Terra Nova, established about 1891 and once called Turnover.

Head north along the 2nd Concession E.H.S. At the summit of the hill is yet another good lookout: to the southeast the Oak Ridges can be seen, and to the south, the Mulmur Hills. The swath cut through this is the Pine River Valley, probably caused by meltwater during the last glacial retreat. At the 25th Sideroad Mulmur, turn west into the village of Ruskview.

Continue west on the 25th Sideroad Mulmur to 1st Concession E.H.S. and turn north. Rising to 518 metres (1,700 feet) on the east is Black Bank Hill.

Continue north on Centre Road to the Nottawasaga/Mulmur Townline and head west into the hamlet of Lavender.

Go west again on the Nottawasaga/Mulmur Townline to the 2nd Concession and head north. Continue along the 2nd Concession West (summer road only and very rough) as it zigzags along to the Noisy River Provincial Park. There is a Ministry of Natural Resources access gate on the left.

Noisy River Provincial Park

This 248-hectare (612-acre) nature reserve has been undeveloped to preserve the natural environment, but hiking can be enjoyed without disturbing the flora. There is no parking.

Striped coral root

Primrose Cemetery

Leaving the park, go back to the 2nd Concession, heading north. At the T intersection, turn right and follow the Noisy River into Dunedin.

Dunedin

Once known as Bowerman's Hollow, this hamlet was the first settlement in Nottawasaga Township. In 1833, Israel Bowerman and Archelous Tupper developed several mills. By 1860, the place was thriving, and a Scot, John Carruthers, renamed it Dunedin, after his New Zealand home town, itself named for Dunedin, Scotland, now Edinburgh. Carruthers established a grist mill.

The general store in the village has been in existence since 1860.

While in the village, note the prominence to the north, where turkey vultures often wheel.

Coming out of Dunedin, take the first left, which is Simcoe Road 62, for Glen Huron. You will notice the old mill in the village, as well as a lumber company. Continue through Glen Huron to the north, to Highway 24. Turn left to Devil's Glen Provincial Park.

Devil's Glen Provincial Park

An area of 60 hectares (148 acres), Devil's Glen provides camping, hiking and a variety of activities on 5.5 hectares (13 acres) of the park; the rest is under reserve status.

Devil's Glen is a 152-metre (498-foot) gorge carved by meltwater from the retreating glaciers, and through which the Mad River now runs. At the height of the gorge, Amabel dolomite is visible, with most other strata hidden by talus.

Botanists may note that hart's tongue fern, green spleenwort, northern holly fern, smooth cliff-brake and striped coral-root can be found here.

As always, please be sure to adhere to designated trails, as the steep slopes are sensitive to damage caused by hikers.

There is admission and ample parking.

Go back to Highway 24 and head west into Singhampton.

Singhampton

In the village's heyday, during the late 1800s, there were 250 residents, three stores, two hotels, two carriage shops, grist, woollen, veneer and sawmills. Singhampton was originally known as Mad River Mills. When Josiah R. Sing made his mark on the community after 1846, the village was renamed in his honour. Much of the development of the town was due to Josiah Sing.

Just to the west of the village is a vast network of marshes, the result of poor drainage on the sloping side of the escarpment. Marshes abound from here into the Bruce Peninsula.

Go north out of Singhampton on Nottawasaga Townline, and follow it to the Nottawasaga Lookout.

Nottawasaga Lookout

Classified a nature reserve, Nottawasaga Lookout encompasses 235 hectares (580 acres). Some of the finest examples of crevice caves found along the escarpment are here, some extending 9 metres (29 feet) into the ground. There are also rare orchids and ferns.

There is no parking. Enter the park via the Bruce Trail, which is clearly marked. Please keep to the hiking trails to minimize damage to the sensitive terrain.

From here, backtrack slightly and take the first left, which is Sideroad 26. This is a summer road only. Head east along the 26th Sideroad to the 10th Concession. Turn left at the T to County Road 33 and then head west. Osler Bluff is visible here. County Road 33 becomes County Road 31 at the second bend to the left, leading towards Pretty River Valley Provincial Park.

Eugenia Falls

6

Pretty River Valley to Rocklyn Creek

While the Petun, later the Huron, and then the Chippewa inhabited this land, it was a forest of hardwoods. That changed after 1818, when treaties were signed and the areas now called Osprey, Collingwood, Artemesia and St. Vincent townships were surrendered. White settlers began to move in in the 1840s when Grey County was established, named for the 2nd Earl Grey, British prime minister 1830–34 and also known for an eponymous tea and British condiments from India. (His grandson, the 4th Earl Grey, served as Canada's governor general from 1904 to 1911.) The first wave of settlers was primarily speculators, followed by farmers.

Euphrasia Township was named for an English officer's wife: the name is from the Greek meaning "delight," and delightful this area is. Moose, originally populous in the area, were driven out by logging, which destroyed their shelter, and by the concomitant increase in the numbers of deer, which can live among sparse trees. Wherever there are deer, there will be few or no moose, because of a worm that lives benignly with deer but destroys nerve tissue in moose.

As pressure on their habitat grew, predatory species such as bears, wolves and bobcats took to raiding livestock. Today, there are few predators, though their numbers are increasing as we become more concerned for their preservation.

Settlers first came into the area not by oxcart or foot, but rather by water, travelling up the Beaver River, which was then deep and wide, from Thornbury to Kimberly. The area's many peat bogs once provided the settlers with fuel.

As you travel, you'll note that this is the most northern orchard area of Ontario. Orchards developed about 1850 farther to the north, and off the escarpment, in the Cape Rich area. The crop then as now included apples, peaches, cherries and other small fruits.

The Ministry of Natural Resources has done much to acquire endangered lands from here northward. However, funding allows only for acquisition; there is no budget available to plan and develop the areas—no inventory of just what, exactly, is being protected beyond the major features of the escarpment. So we, in good conscience, couldn't include in our book the many undeveloped escarpment parks from here north.

This tour is probably one of the longest in our guide. It can be travelled in a day, but you won't see much. Four days is ideal.

Skirting the Pretty River Valley on Grey County Road 31, where we left off in the previous chapter, come around Osler Bluff. Many of the roads in this section aren't signed, so you will have to keep your wits about you.

From Grey County Road 31, make a right at the T intersection, and then take the next right. The road here is very steep and there is an excellent view. You will be travelling in a westerly direction, and then south when the road curves to the right. Most of this road borders the Pretty River Valley Provincial Park. We were unable to obtain permission to include this in the guide, though the Bruce Trail does run through the property.

Continue along to Concession 5, which isn't marked. It will be the first paved road to the right. Take this north. You will pass two lovely old graveyards and then come into the village of Gibraltar, which isn't marked and is hardly distinguishable as a village. Turn right onto the gravel road. You'll know you're on the right course if you pass a gravel pit. Continue east to the first road running to the north. It is identifiable by the Bruce Trail blaze on the northwest corner, and by the unassumed road running to the south into the Pretty River Valley Provincial Park. Head north. You will make a very tight turn down Osler Bluff. On the right will be the entrance to the Petun Conservation Area.

Petun Conservation Area

Petun Conservation Area, which may once have served as a native campsite, offers picnicking, hiking, lookouts and interpretive sites. Parking is available.

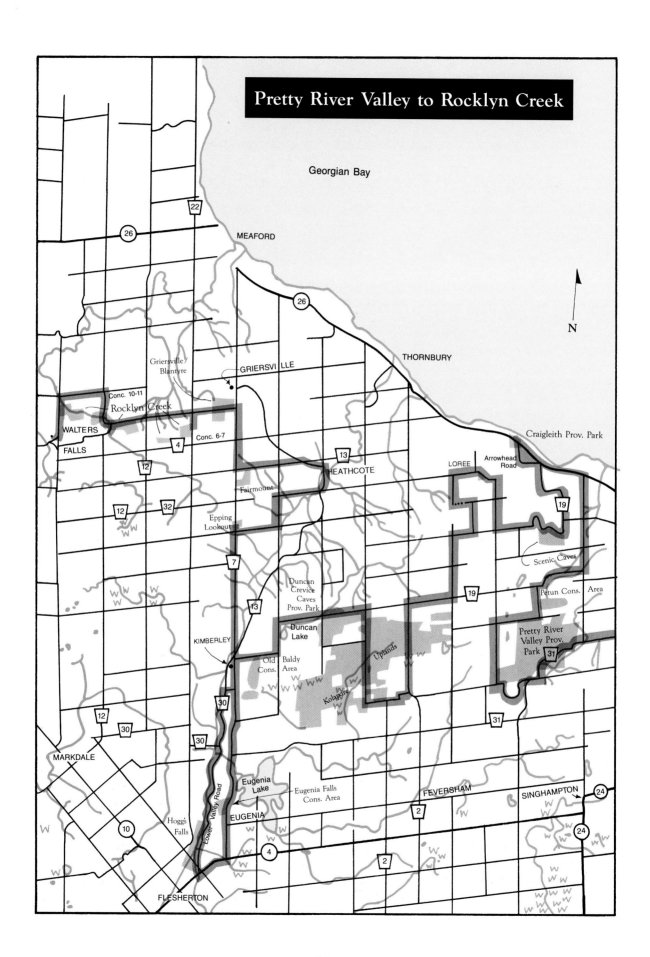

Pretty River Valley to Rocklyn Creek

Georgian Bay

N

MEAFORD

GRIERSVILLE

THORNBURY

Griersville/
Blantyre

Conc. 10-11

Rocklyn Creek

WALTERS
FALLS

Conc. 6-7

HEATHCOTE

Craigleith Prov. Park

Fairmount

LOREE

Arrowhead
Road

Epping
Lookout

Scenic Caves

Duncan
Crevice
Caves
Prov. Park

Petun Cons.   Area

Duncan
Lake

Pretty River
Valley Prov.
Park

KIMBERLEY

Old
Cons.

Baldy
Area

Uplands

Kolapore

MARKDALE

Eugenia
Lake

Eugenia Falls
Cons. Area

FEVERSHAM

SINGHAMPTON

Hogg's
Falls

Lower Valley Road

EUGENIA

FLESHERTON

Continue north. Immediately after Petun Conservation Area is an excellent view of Collingwood.

At the intersection, turn right onto Grey County Road 19. Make a left at the T intersection, continuing north on Grey County Road 19. At Mair Mills, you'll come to a stop sign. Continue north through the stop until you reach Highway 26. Make a left.

As you travel along Highway 6, skirting Nottawasaga Bay, take note of the limestone shelf that forms much of this beach area. There is also a lovely old rail station to the left.

Continue along Highway 26 until you reach Craigleith Provincial Park, on the right.

Craigleith Provincial Park

A recreation escarpment park, Craigleith encompasses 66 hectares (163 acres) for camping and day-use activities. Fishing, swimming, sailboarding, skiing, hiking, boating and spelunking can all be enjoyed here. There is admission.

Take the time to see the historical marker about the Craigleith oil shale works.

Backtrack along Highway 26 to Arrowhead Road, on the right. Follow Arrowhead Road to the south, around the bend and to the east to a T intersection with Grey County Road 19. Turn right. As is all too plain throughout this section, you've entered ski heaven with mushrooming chalets and resorts.

Grey County Road 19 will turn to the east and then south again. Just at the second bend to the east is an enormous sign for the Scenic Caves. Take this turnoff to the right, climbing the escarpment. The Scenic Caves will be on the left.

Scenic Caves and Caverns

This high section of the escarpment was once covered by hardwoods, pine and hemlock. The stone fences throughout the farming area were created when settlers first cleared their lands.

Take the entrance to the Scenic Caves and Caverns. There is admission. The caves are well worth a visit, because the Petun had their villages in this area. One cave remains about 4°C (39°F) throughout the summer and was probably used by natives as a place to store food. The deeper caves retain snow and ice through until fall.

At the place now known as Suicide Point, then as Rock That Stands Out, a legend of lovers evolved. A handsome Erie chief, eager for trade with the Petun, made his way to the Collingwood Mountains to begin negotiations, and here among the Petun he found a maiden known as Leuantido. He loved her dearly, and she him. But Leuantido was forbidden to him, and so they conspired to meet during the evenings among the trees near the caves of the Rock That Stands Out.

Leuantido's brothers, however, discovered the nightly tryst. Angered, they slew the Erie chief. Leuantido was taken back to her tribe. She languished, yearning for the man who had departed to Ekarenniondi. Day after day she would wander through the trees of the Rock That Stands Out, until finally she failed to return.

Her brothers found her body in a fern-shrouded cave beside her lover's resting place. The mists that rise from the escarpment are said to carry the spirits of Leuantido and her Erie lover, so the place is avoided lest those spirits be disturbed.

Here also is the sacred place of Ekarenniondi, where Osctorach (Head Piercer) removed the brains of those who died and were travelling to the Village of the Souls in the west, in order to give them freedom from remembrance of their earthly lives.

You will also have an opportunity to see rare ferns and moss in one of the caves.

Continue west along the road. You'll wind north where there is an excellent lookout, back south and eventually west once more. At the stop sign in Banks, make a right onto Concession 5, which isn't marked, and head north.

For those who are not travelling in a four-wheel-drive vehicle, we urge you strongly to take the first left and then the first left again onto Concession 6, which isn't marked.

If you do have a *good* four-wheel-drive, continue north from Banks. The road will turn to the west, northwest and then west. At this summit you'll catch your first glimpse of the Beaver Valley. Continue west into the forgotten village of Loree. There is a schoolhouse on the right. Take the road across from the schoolhouse to the left, which is Concession 7 and unmarked. The road turns to the east and narrows to resemble a wagon track. It gets worse until you end up climbing over bare shelves of rock just before the road becomes assumed again. Take the first right, which is Concession 6, unmarked.

This is where both our routes meet again. Take the first right and then the first left, which is identifiable by the schoolhouse on the north side of the road. Head south along Concession 7, unmarked, past the old Rock Union church of 1898, to the second right, which has a stop sign. This is Grey County Road 19. Turn right and continue east to Grey County Road 2 and make a left, heading south through the Kolapore Swamp and the village of Kolapore. Take the turnoff to the right at the bend of Grey County Road 2.

Head west. The road turns to the north through the Kolapore Uplands and through Little Germany, which is unmarked.

As you head north, you will drive by a fabulous section of rock riddled with trees, known as Pine Rock. The road here becomes very winding and heads off to the west.

Take the first right, which is Concession 10. There is a magnificent prominence to the right, known as Metcalfe Rock. We'll travel by Mitchell's Falls, although should you wish to take the turnoff to the right into the village, do so. It once had a sawmill, owned by George Walter. After a milling accident in which he lost a hand, Walter sold out to Alex Mitchell, for whom the falls are named.

Otherwise, take the turn to the left onto Collingwood Sideroad 9–10 and head west past Duncan Crevice Caves Provincial Park, another area we were unable to obtain permission to visit. Travel through the village of Duncan.

Duncan

The village was named for Duncan Boles, the first teacher in the school. Once a thriving lumber centre, Duncan had its own post office in 1870, and nine years later a store owned by Alexander McKeown, who was also to become post-master. The business was continued by heirs into the twentieth century.

Sideroad 9–10 will turn off to the south, past Duncan Lake on the left. Take the first right. A road running off to the left opens out to a small parking lot for Old Baldy Conservation Area. To reach the area, you'll have to hike up the Bruce Trail.

Old Baldy Conservation Area

A Niagara Escarpment natural environment area, Old Baldy Conservation Area covers 39.6 hectares (98 acres) on the rim of the Beaver Valley.

The outcrop itself is Amabel dolomite, fractured and beautiful, over which turkey vultures glide all summer long. It also offers an excellent opportunity to study the pre-glacial valley. The chasm here is still in the process of separating from the main escarpment. The drop is 30.5 metres (100 feet). From the prominence on a clear day, you can see to Georgian Bay, 22 kilometres (13 miles) to the north.

Other fissures inland run parallel to the cliff. Over time, the entire dolomite face will break away, exposing the main part of the escarpment.

Along the trail to the outcrop is a lovely carpet of wildflowers, which we hope you won't disturb—constant picking destroys the plants themselves. We also ask you to adhere to the trail to avoid trampling rare species of ferns.

Go back to the car and continue down the steep seasonal road to County Road 13. Turn left into the village of Kimberley, the location of a well-known summer resort, the Talisman Inn, and several attractive shops.

We're at the bottom of the valley now. Continue south along County Road 13 into the village of Eugenia. Follow the signs into Eugenia Falls Conservation Area.

Eugenia Falls and the Village of Eugenia

Like all waterfalls, Eugenia Falls was a sacred place to the bands who lived here. A secret gold mine in the gorge below the 21-metre (70-foot) falls attracted many in the gold madness about 1853. One of the men, a wagonmaker from York, transported his treasure on a four-day journey to his home, dreaming all the while of his fortune. When he arrived and kindled his forge, the noxious fumes from his melting gold nearly killed him. Like all the others, he had dragged home iron pyrite—fool's gold.

If you travel upstream from the falls, you'll find ruins that were probably the house the Purdy brothers, settlers who had obtained the mill rights for the area, built in 1858. The house also served as a post office. The men built a sawmill in 1859 and a flour mill the next year. Later followed a hoop and veneer mill, a sash and door factory (which also made coffins to order), yet another mill, a smithy and lime kiln. Most of these are now gone. The Eugenia House, however, has been in existence since these early times.

Go back to the car and head south on County Road 13 to Highway 4. Turn right. At Beaver Valley Road turn right and then right again to visit Hogg's Falls. There is limited parking here and the hike is a long one, especially when you reach the falls. You'll have to climb down the vertical escarpment face, without aid of any stairs, to the river bottom for the best view. Unless you're fit and an expert climber, we suggest you bypass these falls. In 1895, a hydro generating station was situated here, owned and operated by William Hogg, who had earlier run a sawmill. The ruins still exist.

Continue north along Beaver Valley Road to follow the Beaver River and the lowest point of the valley. You will also come across the operating hydro generating station, fed by a flume from Eugenia Lake.

An excellent canoe route along the Beaver River takes you from Kimberley to Heathcote, more than 20 kilometres (12 miles), in about four hours. Information about the route can be obtained from the Ministry of Natural Resources, Owen Sound, or from Grey-Sauble Conservation Authority, both listed in the back of the book.

The Beaver Valley Road returns you to County Road 13. Turn left, back through the village of Kimberley. Take County Road 7 to the left and head north, climbing the escarpment through the village of Epping and to Epping Lookout.

Epping Lookout

Covering 4.8 hectares (11.8 acres), Epping Lookout provides one of the most scenic sites on the western escarpment rim of the Beaver Valley. There is a small picnic area here, for day use only.

Apple orchard

Backtrack along County Road 7 to the first left and head east. Just before the bridge, take the left-hand turn and follow this road north, around the bend to the east and continue to the T intersection, which is Grey County Road 13. Turn left and head north through the village of Heathcote.

Heathcote Griersville Road

This existing stretch of road covers the only remaining section of the Old Mail or Government Road, the first road through the district, built sometime after the survey of 1836. The road continues to the northwest into the village of Griersville.

Two miles south of the village of Heathcote, in what was known as Williamstown, was an area where Peter Wabash, a Chippewa, made his winter camp every year. Known as the old chief, he lived to be over 100, with hair as dark as during his youth.

The village of Heathcote dates from sometime prior to 1854 and had a school, a smithy, one of the largest general stores in the province, and churches and annual fairs.

Just past the bridge, take the left turn that follows the Old Mail Road, and then take the left fork to the west, to the village of Fairmount, site of the first tavern of Euphrasia

Township, known as Duke's Tavern, where the local council met after 1854.

At Fairmount, turn right onto County Road 7. Follow this north to the St. Vincent/Euphrasia Townline, which will be the second left. There is a church on the east side of the road. Turn left so you are heading in a westerly direction.

The first intersection is a paved road. Turn left here and travel to the Bruce Trail, identifiable by the stiles on the east and west sides of the road. If you feel energetic, we urge you to pull off the road and take a hike to the Griersville Natural Area.

Griersville Natural Area

A series of undeveloped lands totalling 155.2 hectares (383 acres), the Griersville Natural Area not only overlooks a fine section of drumlin fields, but also contains significant springs, the headwaters for the Minniehill Creek, which in turn feeds the Bighead River. To reach one set of springs, hike along the Bruce Trail for about 1.5 kilometres (0.9 miles) to the east. The other set of springs is to the southwest, about 1 kilometre (0.6 miles) in, at the base of the escarpment at a prominent V in the valley.

Hogg's Falls

Head out to the St. Vincent/Euphrasia Townline, turn left and take the second left. Just before the bend of the road, you should see the Bruce Trail to the left. The white blaze is difficult to find, on a large stump. This is the first section of Rocklyn Creek Natural Area we will visit.

Rocklyn Creek

The natural area itself covers 191.6 hectares (473 acres) of escarpment, woodlands, fields and part of the Rocklyn Creek, and is a contact region between the Bighead Drumlin Field and the Niagara Escarpment. There are also sinkholes here, as well as numerous springs that feed into Rocklyn Creek. Many of the crevices are filled with snow in June. The large boulders probably originated from the north shore of Georgian Bay, carried here during the last glacial period.

Atop the escarpment, you are afforded a view to the northern rim of the Bighead Valley and a terrific view of the Bighead Drumlin Fields. On a clear day you can see the mesa of dolomite to the northeast in the Meaford Tank Range area.

To get to this section, hike in from the Bruce Trail to the left about 3 kilometres (1.8 miles). As this is an undeveloped area with sensitive flora, we ask you to adhere to the Bruce Trail.

To get to the other interesting section of Rocklyn Creek, hike back to your car and cross to the Bruce Trail on the east side of the road. This hike is about 3 kilometres (1.8 miles) and heads in a northwesterly direction. Once you reach the old logging road, continue to the east.

Your destination is the end of the road and the Marshall Woods, one of the last areas of virgin hardwood in Southern Ontario.

Hike to your car and drive out to the St. Vincent/Euphrasia Townline. Turn left and then right as the road turns to the north. Take the first left, through the village of Strathnairn, across the bridge and make the left immediately after the bridge. Keep to the right and follow the road into the village of Walters Falls.

7

Walters Falls to Colpoy's Range

Northward from Owen Sound the terrain of the Niagara Escarpment becomes more and more rugged, wild in its beauty, full of native lore and history and tragedy.

By 1836, under the Sauking Treaty, most everything south of Owen Sound had been surrendered to the Crown. This was aboriginal land where the passenger pigeon flew through dense hardwood country, where bears were so abundant that the first settlers caught them in deadfalls to prevent loss of livestock, and where trees often measured 1.8 metres (6 feet) in diameter. The forests were maple, beech and elm, scattered with hemlock, basswood, ash, oak, pine and cedar. Many of the lookouts along the Bruce Trail are the same ones used by natives for thousands of years.

The tour should take from one to two days.

Walters Falls

The village is named for John Walter, a native of Somersetshire, England. When Walter arrived in 1850, there were several falls on the stream that ran through his property, and over the next five years he built a sawmill, grist mill and carding mill. A sawmill built in 1868 was destroyed by fire, and the ruins remain to walk through.

By 1867, a feed mill, later known as the Imperial Flour Mill, was erected. It burned down in 1923, was rebuilt and is now owned by Walters Falls Milling Company. The woollen mill still standing was constructed in 1877.

At the corner of Front and Victoria streets was the first hotel, the Queen's, where the post office was also situated. There was, in addition, a lime kiln in the area.

By the turn of the century, more than 250 people lived in the village, with two barbers, four blacksmiths, a cabinetmaker, a butcher, shoemaker, tailor, undertaker and harness shop, with a fine fair held every year.

To reach one set of falls, turn right at Front Street. After viewing the falls, continue out of Walters Falls along County Road 4 to County Road 29. Turn right and make your first left onto the Sydenham/Holland Townline, which, like so many roads in this area, is not marked. At the third right, turn north. At the top of the hill, on the left, is an access road to Spey River Forest East.

Spey River Forest East

A natural area of 229 hectares (565 acres), the forest includes part of the Bighead Drumlin Field, which comprises more than 300 drumlins.

If you hike along the access road, you will see an early pioneer cabin, probably a home on an unproductive farm.

For the amateur naturalist, this is an area of ferns, orchids, herbaceous plants, and many birds and waterfowl. As there are no official trails, we ask you to go with care. There is no parking.

Hike back to your car and continue north to the T intersection at County Road 18. Turn right to Bognor Marsh Management Area on the left.

Bognor Marsh Management Area

The area was named for the village lying to the southeast of the wetlands. Originally known as Sydenham Mills, the village had a sawmill and flour mill on the Bighead River. This was later joined by a basket and broom factory, shingle mill, post office, general store, smithy and carriage shop, churches and schools.

The management area encompasses 620 hectares (1,531 acres) of headwaters for the Bighead River Watershed and is a paradise for wildlife. The MNR has reforested part of these lands, enhancing the wildlife habitat. Ducks Unlimited has restored waterfowl habitat, and because of that, controlled hunting is allowed, according to their promotional literature, "to protect resident waterfowl populations and maintain a high-quality hunting experience."

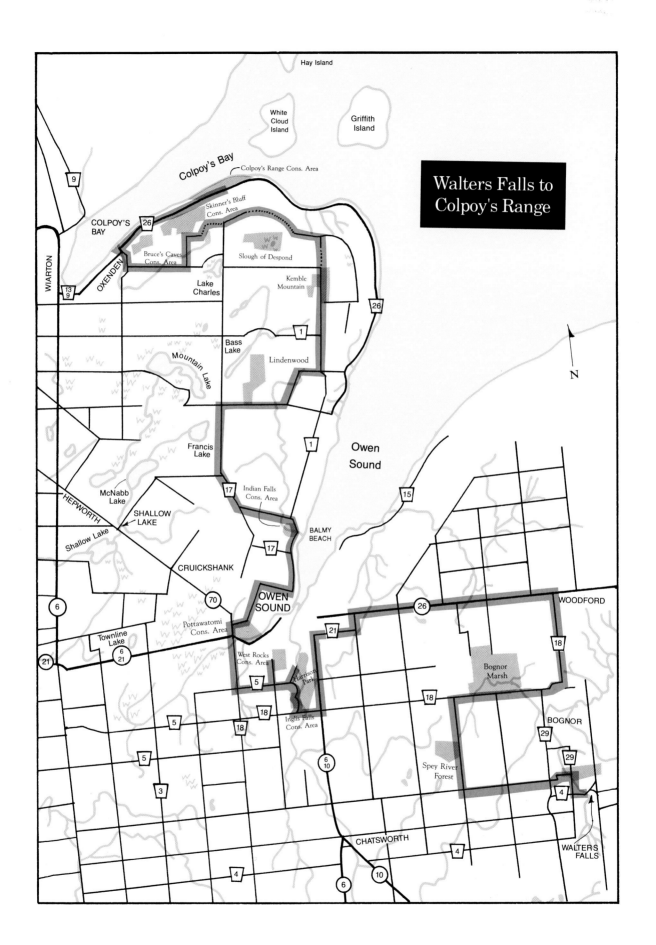

Walters Falls to Colpoy's Range

Hiking, cross-country skiing, snowshoeing and snowmobiling are also allowed here. I'd prefer that snowmobiles, a menace to animals and vegetation, be confined to recreational areas away from natural habitats.

If you are a lover of wetlands and varied terrain, this area is sure to please.

Go back to County Road 18 and continue east to the fourth intersection where it comes to a T. Turn left and continue north along County Road 18 up to Woodford at the intersection of Highway 26 and County Road 18. Should you wish to see the village of Woodford, take the road immediately to your north, which loops back to Highway 26.

Woodford

Situated on the Old Mail Road, Woodford was the site of Sydenham Township's first post office in 1852 and a stopping place for coach passengers. A log hotel also served as post office and school, on the site of the present hotel. Woodford also had a thriving pottery business, as well as a tannery, cabinetmaker, shoemaker, grist mill and sawmill.

Although the first churches in most nineteenth-century settlements were Methodist, Woodford's was Quaker, built in 1866 and torn down in 1933.

Head west out of Woodford along Highway 26 to Grey County Road 21. Turn right and head out to Highways 6 and 10. Turn left and follow Highway 6 to Rockford, where County Road 18 intersects. Turn right at the flashing lights. Inglis Falls Conservation Area will be on the right.

Inglis Falls Conservation Area

A delightful hoax was perpetrated at Inglis Falls in 1876 with the visit by Lord and Lady Dufferin to Owen Sound. The Sydenham River had been very low that year because of drought, so the falls were anything but spectacular. Townspeople, determined to impress the vice-regal couple, secretly dammed the river farther upstream. The waters were released when the mayor gave his cue, and Lord and Lady Dufferin witnessed a spectacle such as the town had never seen: the falls were at their best. However, much to the mayor's chagrin, the guests lingered, so the dignitaries had to be urged away before the torrent abated. Lord and Lady Dufferin departed, duly impressed.

A man named Herriman established the first mill above the falls in 1842, with a second mill built in the same year by a fellow known as Stephens, and another by George Elliot. Elliot later sold to W. C. Boyd and Peter Inglis, the latter gaining possession in 1845. Under Inglis, a flour mill was operated, with a dam above the falls. A sawmill and carding mill were later added.

The block formation of the falls, unusual for escarpment falls, is a result of temperature extremes that cause fissures in the dolomite. The fissures are then exposed to water, which freezes and thaws, creating dynamic hydraulic forces that pry apart the stone. Harder than the underlying sand and limestone, the dolomite breaks off in blocks. Such erosion becomes more visible to the north, particularly at Bruce National Park along the overhang areas.

The conservation area encompasses part of the Sydenham River as well as 200 hectares (494 acres) of wooded valleyland, forming a greenbelt almost 8 kilometres (5 miles) long. This is also a Niagara Escarpment nodal park.

Hiking can be enjoyed along a well-developed trail system. Washrooms, a picnic area and parking are available. There is no admission.

To see the ruins of the old Inglis mill, travel down to Harrison Park and hike along the trails on the east side of the river. To get there, continue through Inglis Falls Conservation Area to the north. You'll see springs to the left of the road. Turn right at the bottom of the hill onto First Street East, which leads directly into Harrison Park. There is no admission, lots of parking, picnic facilities, pedal boats, a small aviary, a refreshment stand, a playground, washrooms and camping.

After Harrison Park, make a left onto First Street East and follow it out of Owen Sound to where it becomes Second Avenue East. You'll come to an intersection where a sign for Walker Park is posted. Turn right here and head north to West Rocks, on the right.

West Rocks Conservation Area

Located on the brow of the escarpment, West Rocks Conservation Area covers 58.4 hectares (144 acres) in three separate parcels; we will visit the largest.

Primarily dolomite, much of the rock has formed excellent crevice caves. There is also a fine second-growth maple-beech forest here, as well as many species of rare ferns. Ruffed grouse are abundant, as are illegal hunters. Go with care.

The view of Owen Sound and the harbour is breathtaking even on the dullest days.

To reach the area, you'll be required to park in the small parking area provided and hike back to the Bruce Trail, on the east side of the road, south of the parking lot.

Backtrack and make a right at the intersection. At the first stop sign, turn right onto Grey County Road 18, heading north into the village of Springmount. Go through Springmount. To the right, on Highway 70, is the entrance to the Pottawatomi Conservation Area.

Bruce's Caves

Pottawatomi Conservation Area

A Niagara Escarpment natural area, Pottawatomi Conservation Area covers 116 hectares (286 acres) of waterfalls, rivers, streams, open fields and forests. Excellent hiking and picnicking are possible.

Samuel Jones had a sawmill here at Jones Falls, built in 1880 at the bridge of the north side of the road. Logs used to be piled in what is now Conklin's lumber yard and from there hauled to Owen Sound.

From Pottawatomi Conservation Area, continue north along Highway 70 to the Derby/Sarawak Townline and turn right. There is a drive-in theatre on the southwest corner. Take the first left, which is West Street. West Street bends to the east and becomes 24th Street. Stay on this paved road. Then 24th Street bends, becoming 4th Avenue West. Make a left at 23rd Street West and then left onto East Sargeant Parkway. We will not be travelling into Owen Sound proper, but should you wish to, by all means visit.

Owen Sound

The sound is really a bay, named for Admiral Sir Edward William Campbell Rich Owen, who was exceedingly careful to take many soundings during his night voyage into the body of water in 1815.

In 1842, a man named Stephens, who later built a mill at Inglis Falls, arrived from Toronto at Owen Sound (then known as Sydenham) aboard a 15-ton schooner called the *Fly*. Across the bay, the Chippewa Chief Nawash kept a village that had been cleared from the forest by the government after the Sauking Treaty had granted the Crown all land south of Owen Sound. To Nawash and his people the place was known as Nah-she-tigwayog-weequaid, or "bay of two rivers."

Owen Sound, supported primarily by the Inglis mills and those run by other men, had prospered so much that by 1844 a regular steamer included Owen Sound on its route between Sturgeon Falls and Sarnia. This was important because there were few roads into the backwoods, and the majority of trade and travel was done by water.

By 1853, Owen Sound was a county seat, and official buildings were erected. The Chippewa, however, were faring less well than the settlers. After a government meeting in 1855 failed to address their concerns over payments, land and hunting rights, the chiefs in full war paint marched in protest through the streets of Owen Sound. But by 1857 Nawash had surrendered his lands and moved with his people to Cape Croker, north of Owen Sound, near Colpoy's Bay. That settlement still exists as a reserve.

Owen Sound prospered. The company that erected the dry dock was organized in 1875. By then access was relatively easy to other centres via the Toronto and Sydenham Road, Garafraxa Road and Durham Road.

Visitors may be interested in the Grey County Court House, completed in 1853, on 3rd Avenue East north of 12th Street, and the town hall, built in 1870.

Continue along East Sargeant Parkway, which is also Grey County Road 1, into Balmy Beach. Indian Falls Conservation Area is on the left.

Balmy Beach

James McLaughlan, a businessman with a different vision than most, established in Balmy Beach in 1899 a pavilion and auditorium to entertain the thousands of tourists who came from Owen Sound by steamer. By 1900, his trade was doing so well that road tours were booked throughout the season. Two years after that, he opened the King's Royal Hotel, the first luxury resort in Ontario. It was not a success and McLaughlan was forced to close in 1914.

Indian Falls Conservation Area

Managed by the Grey-Sauble Conservation Authority, the 12 hectares (29 acres) of parkland were developed from a reclaimed gravel pit. Indian Falls, typical escarpment falls, is 15 metres (49 feet) high and has clearly exposed the soft layers of Queenston shale.

A baseball diamond, shuffleboard courts, tennis courts and a children's playground are all located in the adjacent Lindlue Hurlbut Memorial Park. In the conservation area itself are picnic tables, washroom facilities and a walking trail approximately 0.8 kilometres (½ mile) long. This trail leads to Indian Falls.

For many years this was the favourite summer village of the Nawash Chippewa and was called Drum Falls. When Europeans settled the area, a fellow known as Wilson had a flour and grist mill west of the recreation area, about 1877. The first sawmill was built by a man by the name of Malard, just below the old Balmy Beach bridge, about 1863. Although the building suffered damage in a flood and a fire, it was restored several times and is still in use today.

Continue north on County Road 1 to Acres Road and turn left. At County Road 17, make a right and drive through the Glen Management Area. As this is a difficult area to get into, as well as being ecologically sensitive, we'll forgo a visit and travel farther north along County Road 17 and make a right at Concession 15–16, which is not marked. You'll know you're on the right track by the sign on the southwest side of the road marking Lindenwood Management Area. About 4.5 kilometres (2.8 miles) on the left side, across the road from the old schoolhouse, is a Bruce Trail entrance. The blaze is difficult to see. We suggest you find a safe,

convenient place to park and use the Bruce to go into Lindenwood Management Area, travelling north.

Lindenwood Management Area

These 242 hectares (597 acres) of natural environment lands provide an opportunity to study the effects of the last glacial period. Striations in the rocks near Concession 15–16 are evidence of glacial ice scraping. Also, from the brow of the escarpment there is an excellent view of the glacial Lake Algonquin plain, which lies to the east, and the drumlin, which abuts the escarpment base.

Hike back along the Bruce to your car. From here continue east along Concession 15–16, across the bridge, to the first intersection and turn left. This is a narrow gravel road, somewhat hidden. As you travel northward you'll have a good view of the escarpment face to the left.

At the T intersection, turn right onto Keppel/Sarawak Townline, which is also unmarked, and then left onto hard-surfaced County Road 1 to the village of Kemble. Continue north through Kemble onto the gravel road, unmarked, and into the Kemble Mountain Management Area.

Kemble Mountain Management Area

Covering 136 hectares (336 acres), this natural environment area is accessible from the Bruce Trail just to the right of Sideroad 40-41. The hike is about 2 kilometres (1.8 miles) and affords a view of the Pyette Hill outlier, as well as a secondary escarpment branching off to the northeast.

At the base of the south-facing escarpment are two lakes that are the headwaters for Indian Creek. The shelf between the two scarps is Manitoulin dolomite, ranging from 1 to 3 kilometres (0.6 to 1.8 miles) in width, and east of Kemble Mountain are cliffs up to 30 metres (98 feet) in height. The mountain itself is a headland separating two re-entrant valleys, Colpoy's Bay and Owen Sound. The orientation of indentations, contours and surface deposits follows the direction of ice movement, evidence of terrific erosion.

Go back to the car and travel north to the first intersection and continue north along the seasonal road. Some of this is very steep, very rugged and very beautiful.

At the next T intersection, keep to the left. Continue west after the stop sign, and turn right at the next intersection onto another seasonal road, and then left.

Here we skirt the Slough of Despond, not visit it, as it's on private property and the area is difficult, perhaps even dangerous, to reach because there are no benchmarks through the woods. This is an important area: the slough is an impounded lagoon of glacial Lake Algonquin. Cobble bars built up by wave action at the mouth of the bay to the north

Autumn

closed the area in. Then, as the meltwaters receded a total of 61 metres (200 feet), the slough was completely cut off.

To the northwest of the slough is Esther's Bluff, of Paleozoic origin, still eroding, like so many of the exposed areas of the escarpment.

We ask you to proceed with extreme care. The road is rough, precipitous and very narrow. Should you wish to pick up the Bruce Trail, the rigorous hike is worthwhile—there are swamp rose, sweet gale, buttonbush, spicebush, twayblade, round-leaved orchids, water willows and myriad ferns.

As the road begins to dip to the south, you'll find Bruce Trail blazes to the right. Here you can follow the Bruce along the top of Skinner's Bluff.

Skinner's Bluff Management Area

This natural area of 249.2 hectares (615 acres) hugs the brow of the escarpment where it overlooks Colpoy's Bay. The bluff is a promontory separating the two re-entrant valleys of Colpoy's Bay and Owen Sound.

The vegetation that clings here grows because of the microclimates created in the fissures, not unlike the alvars on the western side of the Bruce Peninsula.

If you look across Colpoy's Bay, originally We-shuskweequaid ("muskrat"), to White Cloud Island you will be looking at another ancient battleground. To the east, on a clear day, you may be able to see the cobble bar in the bay.

Continue along this road, which turns sharply to the east where it is no longer seasonal, and then to the south. At the first stop sign, turn right onto the paved road. You pass Gleasonbrook Pottery just before a T intersection. Turn right and follow the road into the village of Oxenden.

Oxenden

The Jesuits had a mission here in the seventeenth century. In 1856, the first settlers began arriving. By 1861, the Chippewa had lost Oxenden, after at least 200 years in the area. Whites auctioned the land even before Chief Nawash had released it.

One of the early settlers was a Scot named Bruce who purchased Crown land and built a cabin near a cave in the rock. The land was later sold to Henry Loney, though Bruce kept the cabin and cave. Bruce's Cave near Oxenden is named for him, as are Bruce's Mines on the north shore.

Take County Road 26 to the right. Bruce's Caves Conservation Area is immediately on the right at the bend. It's easy to miss, so keep your eyes open.

Bruce's Caves Conservation Area

This natural area covers 51 hectares (126 acres) and offers

Mallard ducks, female (at left) and male

picnic tables and hiking, as well as the famed caves themselves. There is parking.

The caves are the result of wave action from glacial Lake Algonquin, as well as seepage from ground and surface waters that dissolved limestone in stratification lines. This left the harder dolomite behind, though softer sections are strewn across the cave floors. The natural columns were created when large sections of dolomite snapped away.

Continue east along County Road 26, hugging Colpoy's Bay, to Colpoy's Range and Lookout Conservation Area, on your left.

Colpoy's Range and Lookout Conservation Area

This is a recreation area of 7.7 hectares (19 acres) sandwiched between the Georgian Bay shoreline and County Road 26. There are limited picnic facilities here, as well as the lookout, privies, barbecue sites and two historical plaques, describing the loss of the *Jane Miller* in 1881 and the formation of Skinner's Bluff. The wreck of the *Jane Miller* was never found, and why she disappeared no one ever knew.

Please note: the water at the lookout site is contaminated. *Do not drink it.*

The area is located on a shingle beach of Queenston shale, created by Lake Algonquin. There is also an excellent opportunity here to see the secondary Manitoulin scarp running below Skinner's Bluff.

For a scenic wrap-up to this tour, follow County Road 26 right around the cape to its intersection with County Road 1, and down to Owen Sound. It's a picturesque drive with the cliffs looming on the right and the bay on the left. You'll pass through several sleepy villages, such as Big Bay, Pyette Point and Hogg.

Escarpment cliffs, Bruce Peninsula

THE BRUCE PENINSULA

This region, specifically Bruce County, the subject of the following two tours, was left to the native peoples while the rest of the escarpment underwent settlement. In the early days it was known as the Saugeen Peninsula and then the Indian Peninsula.

Jesuit missions reached the Bruce in 10 locations in the early 1600s. By 1650, they and the Petun were driven away by the Iroquois.

When Methodist ministers came into what was later known as the Queen's Bush, in 1834, the western side of the land was more easily passable. Settlement began only after the 1847 survey.

Pennsylvania Dutch Mennonites and a rough lot of evicted Highlanders who spoke only Gaelic moved in next. Both groups settled mostly to the west, leaving the rugged terrain of the escarpment untouched. Even the railway hugged the western shore, going only as far as Southampton, as it does today.

Settlement was short-lived. The call of the West and the prospects of fertile lands attracted many pioneers, so the population declined. Fish resources were harvested in obscene amounts; large-scale logging left the land almost barren. The lake played a greater part in the settlement of the region; newcomers used it as the natives had, for transportation, as the few roads were virtually impassable.

Drainage and irrigation schemes were undertaken to provide arable land, but as the soil proved shallow and costs exorbitant, many of the vast wetlands of the Bruce were left untouched. In some places, excessive drainage was destructive to the ecosystem.

Slowly, the Bruce has rejuvenated. It now displays rare pockets of orchids and breathtaking ferns. Because of the cliffs on the eastern shore, a diverse natural population thrives on the western shore. Parts of the peninsula are less susceptible to summer frosts than more southerly regions, owing to the moderating influence of the lake on either side. The western shore of the lake is sunnier in the summer, even when clouds form a few miles inland. In winter the same effect causes heavier snowfalls on the lee side because of prevailing winds.

Fragile wildflowers, orchids especially, abound to the west. The frail long-bracted orchid exists in just one known area—and then only three plants. A subdivision is planned for the very spot where these rare beauties grow.

Many of the reserves and natural environment areas on the east cannot handle increased public traffic, even though the Bruce Trail does run through, so we have omitted many of these parks from our tour.

Alvar on the western side of the Bruce Peninsula

8

Southern Bruce Peninsula Loop

This tour takes you in a loop around the southern part of the peninsula, starting at Wiarton and heading around the eastern edge, then down the western side.

The conveniences available south of Wiarton are absent here. We suggest you plan picnics. Hiking gear is a must. As always, we ask you to go with care.

Allow yourself two to three days to tour the area, especially if you're a hiking and nature enthusiast.

Continue from County Road 26 into Wiarton.

Wiarton

Sheltered in Colpoy's Bay is the town of Wiarton. James Lennox built the first shanty in 1866. Settlement followed, and for years Wiarton was the only market town in the area, though there were no landing facilities. As a result, Wiarton originally hugged the hill where Gould Street crosses Division Street. At this intersection was B. B. Miller's hotel and post office of 1868, later followed by stores owned by John Hodgins and David Dinsmore. The construction of wharves and mills caused businesses to migrate down to Berford Street, leaving Gould Street to become residential. The town continued to grow, with the expectation of a railway connection. However, the Stratford & Lake Huron Railway was unable to carry out its plans, and years passed before the Grand Trunk came into Wiarton in 1881.

A tornado devastated the town in 1892. All but two dwellings were demolished, the sawmill roof was torn off, and the skating rink, public baths, a boathouse and stables were levelled.

From County Road 26, which becomes County Road 13 as you enter Wiarton, make a right at the first stop sign. There is a gas station on the northwest corner. You are now on Highway 6. Follow Highway 6 to the north. On the right is Spirit Rock Conservation Area.

Spirit Rock Conservation Area

According to Spirit Rock's legend, the daughter of a chief was carried off by an eastern nation and forced into slavery. To ease her soul of sorrow, she sang hauntingly and sweetly, thus enamouring the chief. His small kindnesses endeared him to her, and gradually she came to love him. But to love her from afar wasn't what the chief wanted, so he released her from bondage and took her for his wife.

His people were furious. They plotted against him and killed him. She escaped, wandering back to her own people, who exiled her because she had willingly become the wife of their foe and dishonoured her people. Distraught, she hid in the rocks till nightfall and then threw herself from the heights into the bay. Her face is said to stare from the cliff, engraved there by the power of the manitous.

Spirit Rock Conservation Area covers 86.4 hectares (213 acres) from the summit to the foot of the escarpment. On the summit are glacial erratics, crevasses and large depositions of rock. Christmas fern and holly fern can be found. A swamp exists in the northwestern section.

At the entrance, the ruins of the McNeill estate are accessible. The stone mansion, built in 1881, had 17 rooms and was named Corran, after McNeill's childhood home in Ireland. A new wing was added in 1910, with a conservatory, library, kitchen and three bedrooms above. There were also two cottages on the property, one of which was the McNeill home while Corran was under construction.

McNeill was a lover of gardens. His rose gardens were famous: he gave every departing guest a single bloom from one of his more than 500 bushes. The orchard was substantial, with 200 apple trees and over 50 pear trees. Many of the roses and fruit trees still grow here.

When McNeill died in 1930, his son squandered his inheritance. When he died in 1956, the estate was left to his

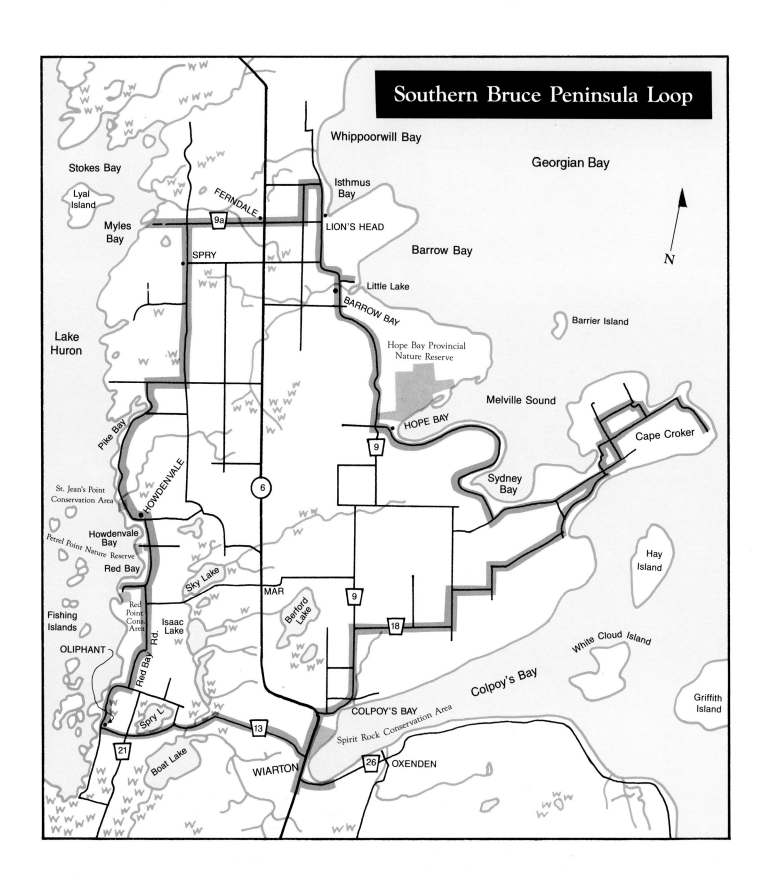

Southern Bruce Peninsula Loop

Stokes Bay

Lyal Island

Myles Bay

FERNDALE

9a

SPRY

Whippoorwill Bay

Isthmus Bay

LION'S HEAD

Barrow Bay

Little Lake

BARROW BAY

Georgian Bay

N

Barrier Island

Lake Huron

Pike Bay

St. Jean's Point Conservation Area

HOWDENVALE

Howdenvale Bay

Petrel Point Nature Reserve

Red Bay

Fishing Islands

OLIPHANT

Red Point Cons. Area

Isaac Lake

Red Bay Rd.

Sky Lake

MAR

Berford Lake

Hope Bay Provincial Nature Reserve

Melville Sound

HOPE BAY

9

Sydney Bay

Cape Croker

Hay Island

9

18

White Cloud Island

Griffith Island

Spry L.

Boat Lake

21

13

WIARTON

COLPOY'S BAY

Colpoy's Bay

Spirit Rock Conservation Area

26

OXENDEN

6

housekeeper, Sally Simmons, who in turn sold it in 1960. By 1970, the property had been sold to the Sauble Valley Conservation Authority. Vandals burnt Corran, destroying this wonderful legacy.

Picnic facilities, trails and washrooms are all available. Spirit Rock itself is accessible via a circular metal staircase that ascends the escarpment.

Continue north along Highway 6 to Bruce County Road 9 and head off to the right. Follow the road into the village of Colpoy's Bay, settled about 1856. Inhabitants hoped their village would grow the way Wiarton did, but it remains now much as it was then.

From Colpoy's Bay, travel north on County Road 9. Make a right at County Road 18. There is a signpost marking the direction to Purple Valley. Take the second left, through the village of Purple Valley, now just a ghost town.

Take the first right, marked by a reserve sign. This is a gravel road. From here take the next left. You'll be travelling north. The road turns to the east into the Cape Croker Reserve.

Cape Croker—The Chippewas of Nawash

A result of the Peter Jones Treaty, the Cape Croker Reserve was established in 1857 as a homeland for the Chippewas of Nawash. Pushed farther and farther from the vast lands they had wandered, the band managed to retain this peninsula. Some, however, longed for their original lands, but when such lands came up for auction, the natives were barred from purchase. Promised annuities were slow in coming. Princess Naw-Nee-Ban carried the plight of her people to Queen Victoria, and the Prince of Wales was even petitioned during his visit to Collingwood—all to no avail. The annuities did come, but in their own good time.

Rev. James Atkey arrived in 1853, and under his direction a church and school were built. Three years later the Jesuits established a mission, perhaps for the second time (there is speculation that their first mission here was established in the seventeenth century), on the site of the present St. Mary's Church.

From the 1880s, fishing, farming and lumbering were the chief means of subsistence, augmented by sugar-making. The Chippewa, a hunter-gatherer people, were not attracted to agriculture, nor was the terrain suitable for cultivation. Perhaps because of native reluctance to dominate the land, Cape Croker remains a haven for waterfowl and wildlife.

A cairn was erected to Chief Nawash, in recognition of his service during the War of 1812 and his contributions to the band. *Nawash* means "a tree bending in the wind, but not yielding."

Before touring the cape, you should check in with the band office as a courtesy—these are private lands.

Cape Croker offers those with an interest in geology a good opportunity to see storm beaches from Pine Tree Point to Cove of Cork Bay, where the lighthouse is situated.

The roads are unnamed. Stay sharp, though it's not easy to get lost.

Entering the cape, you will travel between King's Point Bluff to the right and Jones Bluff to the left. Make a left at the T intersection and keep to the shore. You'll pass the band office on the left-hand side. The road turns to the left. There is a United church on the corner, where you make a right. The road eventually curves to the left. At the next intersection, turn right and follow this road out to the cape, over the wooden crossing and around the bend to the right. At the end of this road is the lighthouse. Between June and July the entire stretch of road is lined with columbine and Indian paintbrush.

If you have the patience, and sit still long enough, you will see hummingbirds zoom in to feed from the columbine. They always give a spectacular show and are quite unafraid of humans.

From here, backtrack to the intersection just past the wooden crossing and make a right. At the next intersection turn left, and then right at the following one. This will take you back to familiar territory at the next intersection, where you will turn right, hug Macgregor Harbour and come back out to the intersection at the United church. Turn left here.

The land outside the village of Cape Croker becomes extraordinarily flat and is dubbed The Prairie. Before you is the imposing rise of Jones Bluff. The road circles to the north of the bluff.

As you rise up the escarpment, a sign directs you to the right for the reserve craft store. Make this right. Pass through the gates to Cape Croker Park. At the time we prepared this book, there was no admission.

The road twists and winds through lovely woodland, round Sydney Bay. When you come to a circle, stay to its right and do not ascend the escarpment. From here, continue to skirt the base of Sydney Bay Bluff, eventually leaving the reserve.

Your path will take you round another bay, this time Hope Bay. The bluffs that loom to the north are part of the Hope Bay Provincial Nature Reserve.

At the foot of the bay, the road will turn off to the east and intersect with County Road 9. Turn right onto County Road 9.

At the next intersection we suggest you find a convenient place to park and hike to the east along the Bruce Trail. Your destination is Hope Bay Provincial Nature Reserve.

Hope Bay Provincial Nature Reserve

Also known as Cathedral Woods, this area is a rocky forest where trees grow on a thin layer of soil over dolostone.

The ruins of Corran, once a 17-room mansion

There is also a series of karst formations (collapsed solution caves). Because of this irregular terrain, the area is a haven for numerous plant species, including abundant trillium. Exposed rock provides a rich habitat for rare flora such as walking fern, maidenhair, spleenwort, hart's tongue, long-bracted and showy orchids, and rattlesnake fern. Where the areas have been sheltered, duff has created a rich mulch for other species. As there are many rare species here, we ask you to take care where you walk. You might also be careful yourself: this is rugged terrain.

Farther along the trail is a magnificent lookout, affording an excellent view of Hope Bay and Melville Sound.

Hike back to your car. Continue north along County Road 9 and into Barrow Bay, settled about 1874. Turn right after the bridge in Barrow Bay, and then take the right fork.

Little Lake

It's not so much Little Lake we've come to see, but Judge's Creek, which empties here. Although it's not a particularly pretty creek now—brown with silt—it was once clear enough to support trout. During settlement, the extensive wetlands which covered the watershed were drained for farmland. According to Ron Reid, an environmental consultant, more than 80 percent of Southern Ontario's wetlands have been destroyed. The remaining wet areas are declining at a rate of 1 to 2 percent a year.

Even if the draining of Judge's Creek area did provide some very fertile arable land, it also destroyed a valuable habitat. Judge's Creek is now little more than a drain carrying silt and agricultural chemical products. Year after year these pollutants spew into Georgian Bay. Within our lifetime the water of Georgian Bay was drinkable, but no longer.

Backtrack to County Road 9 and turn right, heading north into the town of Lion's Head. Descend Bannister's Hill to the shore, where you can look out to Lion's Head Point. At one time the rocky prominence resembled a lion's head, but constant erosion has altered the cliff—you need a good imagination to see the resemblance now.

Lion's Head

In 1875, Lion's Head wasn't much more than a post office and the only store in Eastnor Township. The settlement grew so that by 1879 it contained several homes, two hotels, three stores, a grist mill, planing mill, sawmill, pump factory, a smithy and a population of 100. In three years it doubled in size.

Proximity to navigable waters and a sheltered harbour made Lion's Head a perfect shipping town, with the first wharf built in 1883. Fire destroyed the grist and sawmills in 1889 and these were replaced with a roller-process mill. The boom was brief, and Lion's Head is now principally a tourist town.

At the foot of the hill, take the first road to your left. It is not well marked and therefore easy to miss.

From here we will begin our loop out to the western side of the Bruce.

Take the first left, go south to the stop sign and turn right onto County Road 9. Pass through Ferndale, across Highway 6, past another stop sign and out to Myles Bay. After this stop sign the road is gravel. There are some interesting glacial striations at the end of this road.

Backtrack to the previous intersection. At the stop, turn right. You will head south through the village of Spry, settled sometime after 1870 by people moving from Lion's Head in search of fertile land.

Continue south to the first crossroad. Turn right at the stop, and then take the first left onto a paved road. The route will skirt the body of water known as Pike Bay. Continue to the right at the stop sign in the village of Pike Bay. The road will head south once more.

Before you reach the village of Howdenvale you'll come to St. Jean's Point Conservation Area. It's difficult to find, and at the time of writing there were no signs to mark the area or any parking.

St. Jean's Point Conservation Area

The limestone shore of the 6.1-hectare (15-acre) conservation area was swept by glaciers, clearing debris and scouring the surface. Today, that scouring continues in storms and winter blows. Yet for all of the grinding process, there are no fines (sand, silt and grit produced from the wearing of rocks). The reason is that limestone and dolostone dissolve with little residue, and what little fines there are, are stripped by prevailing winds.

Despite its formidable appearance, the area is alive with insects that have adapted to stormy conditions, as well as a healthy population of waterfowl—cormorants, terns, herons and gulls.

Inland, the limestone pavement changes subtly. Vegetation clings to the rock crevices. This area is known as an alvar. Alvars support plant life with very little soil. In fact, fines that do occur, when blown by the winds, are often caught in the fissures. This habitat is especially inhospitable, with temperatures that range from over 50°C (122°F) to -40°C (-40°F), with daily fluctuations of about 15°.

Despite proximity to the lake, water conditions are also poor here. The rock is either bone dry or covered in standing pools, often for extended, unpredictable periods. Consequently, the nutrient levels range from poisonously concentrated to nonexistent. Cook or freeze. Dehydrate or drown.

Yellow lady's-slipper

Too much food or starvation. There is little here to encourage plant growth.

Yet the plants do grow. The species list comprises 129 varieties of trees, shrubs, herbaceous and other types of plants. Such flora handle harsh conditions efficiently. Some plants tolerate high levels of calcium; others excrete it; all endure low levels of trace nutrients. The plants that do grow here—harebells, bluets, blue-eyed grass—are structured to retard moisture loss. Surprisingly, this area, continuing to Sauble Beach, is a paradise of orchids.

In the crevices themselves you will find mini-ecosystems. Crevices are their own moisture traps, containing damp peaty soils that range 10 to 20° with daily fluctuations of no more than 5 to 8°. Nutrient levels here are relatively stable.

The cedars are the key components in these micro-habitats. The roots bind the soil and absorb nutrients, while the crown shades the crevice, reducing moisture loss. That allows other plants to root. As seasons pass, the cedars and smaller plants create their own soil. Temperature, humidity and soil moisture are all moderated, so among the cedars you find wildflowers, small mammals and birds.

During the winters, the species incapable of enduring the harsh conditions die off. Snow blankets the hummocks, creating an insular effect as well as protecting buds and fragile plant tissues. Those plants that are exposed either die or become stunted. The cedars on an alvar are sometimes as much as 150 years old.

Once you leave St. Jean's Point, continue north and then east as the road bends, into the village of Howdenvale. Take the first right out of the village and head south, then the first right again. There are signs to the right marking the Petrel Point Nature Reserve.

Petrel Point Nature Reserve

Entrance to the 9-hectare (22-acre) reserve is by boardwalk off the gravel road. Please adhere to the trail. Serious damage has resulted because of zealous hikers who have left the trail.

A pocket of fen purchased by the Ontario Federation of Naturalists, Petrel Point is a fragile area where pitcher plants, sundews and bladderwort thrive. These plants do well because of the high alkalinity of the soil—from 7.3 to 8.1—which is directly attributable to the calcareous limestone bedrock that dissolves slowly into groundwater to feed the fen.

The forests of Petrel Point are primarily black spruce, cedar and tamarack, and where the land dries, maple, poplar and black ash. Showy lady's-slipper and bog candles are to be found here, as well as heartleaf, broad-leaved and Loesel's twayblades, grass pink and rose pogonia.

This is also a great place for photography, as many of the plants grow close to the boardwalk—an ideal situation for shutterbugs. But please don't set up in the fen or touch the plants.

Backtrack to the main road we've been travelling, which is still unnamed, and continue south. After the village of Red Bay, turn west onto the gravel road and take it out to the end. Find a convenient place to pull off the road. It's hiking time again.

Reid Point Conservation Area

A fascinating wetland, Reid Point is a difficult place to visit, and we urge you to exercise extreme caution. This route is only for the passionate naturalist. There are no marked trails. The raised bog is nearly impenetrable. Should you get lost, you will find yourself without reference points. It is also fragile, and we ask that you either view the bog from a distance or go with care.

The development of a bog is a slow process. What creates a bog depends greatly on the proliferation of sphagnum mosses. At Reid Point, the bog began as a wet trough between dunes into which acidic duff was deposited. As the layers accumulated, drainage was retarded, concentrating the acidity of the water. That was a perfect recipe for sphagnum moss.

Once the moss took hold, the bog built upon itself, creating a carpet into which shrubs and other plants could take root. Often this layer of vegetation floats atop the acidic water. For this reason a bog is fragile, as well as dangerous—you may think you're on safe ground, only to plunge into cold water. Trying to get out may prove difficult, sometimes impossible. Of course a plunge through the mantle would destroy years upon years of growth.

What to see in a bog? Spring is a time for blooms—lady's-slippers grow in abundance here, as do leatherleaf and Labrador tea, not to mention dwarf lake iris. It is also a haven for sphagnums and lichens as well as birds. Just take your binoculars, pick a safe place and enjoy.

From here, backtrack and continue south along the paved road, and take the first left out to Mar. We begin a fascinating tour along the ancient beaches.

Red Bay Dunes

The dunes that roll through here are the product of time. Originally glacial deposits along the Huron shore, the dunes were carried inland by prevailing winds. Grasses, sedges and other plants took root in the dunes. Small plants created shelter for shrubs, then trees, so that inland the dunes are well canopied. These plants eventually stopped the progression of the dunes, so that now the rolling sands lie parallel to the shore, sometimes only a few metres wide, sometimes over a kilometre. In length, the dunes stretch from Oliphant past Dorcas Bay.

Once you've reached Sky Lake, park in one of the pull-offs near the bridge. Here you'll be able to see the small, secondary escarpment that ranges from 3 to 8 metres (9.8 to 26 feet) in height. It is a significant feature, in that it stops waterflow from its normal westerly flow, and because of that creates a series of shallow lakes (Sky, Isaac and Boat lakes) and wetlands that drain to the south for 24 kilometres (15 miles) before heading west towards Lake Huron. This chain creates a habitat for myriad birds such as the marsh hawk, loon, grebe, and green and great blue herons, to name only a few.

From here, continue east towards Mar over a series of drumlins created during the last ice age. They were covered with Great Lakes–St. Lawrence Forest, but the forest fell to logging.

Backtrack past Sky Lake out to the first left, to head south. The road turns sharply to the west. There is a road marker for this westerly road, Townline, and for the road that continues to the south, Red Bay Road. Make a right at the first stop sign, and then a left at the T intersection. The Fishing Islands are scattered out in the bay ahead.

Fishing Islands

This scattering of islands was surrendered by the natives in 1885 and surveyed in 1900. However, as early as 1831, despite native occupation, Captain MacGregor established himself on one of the islands after discovering the abundant fish in the area. Seized by easy-money fever, he entered into a contract with a Detroit company in 1834 to catch and deliver no less than 3,000 barrels of fish annually, with consideration for surplus. He was to be paid one dollar a barrel, the company to be responsible for cleaning, curing and packing.

And so the rape of the Fishing Islands began. Whitefish and herring, often visible from a height on the mainland as a bright shadow in the water, were caught in quantities difficult to imagine. From one seine net haul 500 to 1,000 barrels could be filled. To expedite this, MacGregor used Main Station Island as a base with homes for his employees and himself, as well as storehouses and other buildings. MacGregor's fortune was taken from him when others discovered the wealth of the Fishing Islands and secured exclusive fishing rights.

Continue south along this road and into the village of Oliphant.

Oliphant

The village was named after Laurence Oliphant, the federal superintendent-general of Indian Affairs in 1854. There were hopes that it would become a business centre, owing to its proximity to the Fishing Islands, but that did not occur, though a post office was built in 1874.

Continue south through the village of Oliphant to the end of the road and turn left. You'll come to a T intersection. From here, either travel north along County Road 21 to County Road 13 and out to Highway 6, or south along County Road 21 to Sauble Beach.

Flowerpot Island, Bruce National Park

9

Northern Bruce Peninsula Loop

Now we enter a place of few roads, massive wetlands, towering cliffs and some of the best scuba diving in Canada.

This was the land of the Chippewa, a place of refuge for many of the persecuted in Wisconsin and other states. European settlement didn't begin until the 1870s, and then none too successfully, as arable land was scarce. There was only one main road at the west of the peninsula, and it wasn't until 1880 that a road was constructed from Lion's Head to Dyer's Bay. Water traffic, however, was active, resulting in numerous lighthouses along both coasts.

With farming poor, many settlers turned to shipping or lumbering, clearing huge tracts of land.

Massasauga rattlesnakes are to be found in the area, so we would caution you to wear thick socks and sturdy hiking boots or shoes. On more than one occasion we have travelled back roads and hiked into the interior and seen no fewer than eight snakes in the space of 300 metres (1,000 feet), though we understand many naturalists have tromped through the Bruce and never found any. Remember, however, they are more afraid of you than you are of them. Caution, respect and common sense will serve you well. A bite is not fatal, but it will make you very ill, and a doctor should be seen as quickly as possible.

Flowerpot Island affords the best show of fairy slippers, also known as Calypso orchids, during the last two weeks of May, though you'll have to work to find them. Do remember to be careful where you walk because these plants are frail.

Birds proliferate, with a range of species to excite any birder. For a more in-depth tour with birds or flowers in mind, contact the Federation of Ontario Naturalists listed in the back of the book. Their tours are excellent.

Although you can do this tour in a day, we recommend three as a minimum—one to get you around, one in Bruce National Park, one in Fathom Five National Park.

We begin our tour at Highway 6, at the Eastnor/Lindsay Townline turnoff to the right, north of Wiarton. Make a

right at Monument Corners, identifiable by the monument on the northeast corner. Take the first left, through what remains of the village of Cape Chin, which had a failed silver mine in the 1890s.

Continue north, past the old church on the left. The paved road bends to the east and then to the north. It's along this road where we have often seen massasauga rattlesnakes between June and July.

After a time the pavement gives way to gravel. Continue north to the T intersection and make a right onto the paved road, which is Dyer's Bay Road. At the next T intersection, turn right. This will lead you into the village of Dyer's Bay. Its post office dates from 1881.

Continue north out of Dyer's Bay. At the forks keep to the right. There will be a sign at some distance notifying you of the Cabot Head lighthouse, and to use the road at your own risk. It's a good road in fair weather, hugging the bay and the bluffs. At some places the cliffs tower 60 metres (200 feet).

The cobble beach, made of limestone coral, brilliant in the sunlight, is known as a storm beach. It's a fascinating place to walk. The cobbles, however, belong to the beach: please do not liberate a few for your collection.

Backtrack to Dyer's Bay when you've reached the lighthouse, return to Dyer's Bay Road and head west out to Highway 6, then north. You'll see Parks Canada signs on the road for Cypress Lake, the campgrounds of Bruce National Park, our next destination.

Bruce National Park

Formerly the Cypress Lake Provincial Park, Bruce National Park encompasses 13,997 hectares (34,586 acres), the majority privately owned. Excellent camping is available, with a total of 242 campsites designed for trailers and tents, with fireplaces and tables on site, as well as toilets and water taps nearby.

For hikers, the Bruce National offers some of the most spectacular walks either on the Bruce Trail, which runs through the park, or the Cyprus Lake Trails. There is also

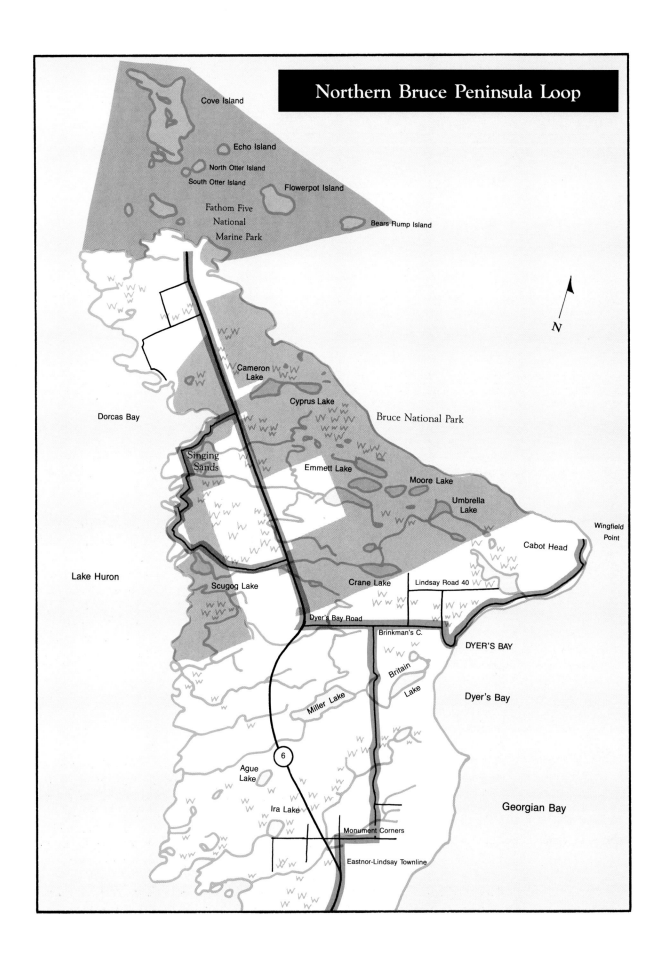

Northern Bruce Peninsula Loop

Cove Island

Echo Island

North Otter Island

South Otter Island

Flowerpot Island

Fathom Five National Marine Park

Bears Rump Island

N

Dorcas Bay

Cameron Lake

Cyprus Lake

Bruce National Park

Singing Sands

Emmett Lake

Moore Lake

Umbrella Lake

Wingfield Point

Cabot Head

Lake Huron

Scugog Lake

Crane Lake

Lindsay Road 40

Dyer's Bay Road

Brinkman's C.

DYER'S BAY

Britain Lake

Dyer's Bay

Miller Lake

6

Ague Lake

Georgian Bay

Ira Lake

Monument Corners

Eastnor-Lindsay Townline

Divers at Tobermory lighthouse, Fathom Five National Marine Park

unsupervised swimming at the Cyprus Lake grounds or on the west side of the Bruce at Singing Sands. You can also boat, fish, cross-country ski, snowshoe and snowmobile. During the evenings, there are interpretive programs.

We recommend that you hike out to the shore to see Marr Lake, an ancient lagoon stranded behind a fabulous cobble bar after Lake Algonquin receded. From here you can hike out to the north to Overhang Point, and then south to Halfway Rock Point, where there is a natural stone arch and sea caves.

Sights here will take your breath away. The trails are well marked and the park staff knowledgeable and helpful. We really recommend you spend a day, or several.

Once you've exhausted yourself with the charms of Bruce National Park, continue north on Highway 6 to Tobermory.

Tobermory

First known as Collins Harbour, Tobermory was renamed after a town in Mull, Scotland. A lumber mill built in 1881 by Maitland and Rixon burned in 1883 and was rebuilt in the same year. A post office also opened in 1883. After six years, the mill was moved to Owen Sound. A lighthouse was erected in 1885 in response to increased shipping and

treacherous shoals around the point. Another mill was built in 1900 by E. M. Meirs and yet another in the following year by Simpson and Culbert.

Tobermory is a delightful place just to wander around. If you're feeling rich, splurge on one of the charters out to Flowerpot Island. Charter companies are listed in For Further Information, or simply look one up in Tobermory.

If you're a diving enthusiast, by all means take advantage of Fathom Five National Marine Park, or, if you are a landlubber like me, book yourself passage on one of the glass-bottom boat tours.

Fathom Five National Marine Park

Canada's first national marine park, Fathom Five covers a freshwater archipelago, known historically as the Cape Hurd Islands. There are a total of 19 islands, encompassing 13,028 hectares (32,191 acres), some still under private ownership. It's a treacherous area. As a result, there are 21 known sail and steam wrecks in the park, accessible only to divers, though you can take a number of glass-bottom boat tours over the wrecks.

One of the more legendary wrecks in this watery park is that of the *Griffon*, the famed vessel that was built for La Salle

Cliffs, Bruce National Park

Sea-cave, Fathom Five National Marine Park

Calypso orchid

One of the largest caves of the area is on the island. There are six campsites, available on a first-come first-served basis, as well as docks, shelter, tables and fireplaces. The lighthouse was erected in 1897.

A visit out to Cove Island will reveal to you the first lighthouse in St. Edmunds Township, erected in 1859.

For divers, there is a list of rules available at the park's Visitors Centre and at the Diver Registration Centre.

Backtrack south on Highway 6 to make the western loop around the northern peninsula. Take the third right, which is the Dorcas Bay Road, out to Singing Sands. Parks Canada signs lead to the area. Once at Singing Sands, we will visit not only this extension of the Bruce National Park, but the Dorcas Bay Nature Reserve.

Dorcas Bay Nature Reserve

Owned by the Federation of Ontario Naturalists, Dorcas Bay fen, 133 hectares (328 acres) in size, protects some of the most unusual plant communities to be found along the Bruce. The entrance is through Singing Sands National Park.

Fascinating to observe is the seiche (the tides of the Great Lakes are caused not by lunar action but by wind) as it rolls up the small stream that meanders along the expansive sand beach. The seiche is so strong that it often reverses the flow of the stream, sometimes flooding the bridge and the entire inland meadow.

There are three routes to follow in the reserve. The most difficult, fragile and wettest is the inland one to the east. A wet dune area that gradually rises into forests, this section covers one-third of the reserve. Past Highway 6, where the dunes continue, is the ancient beach of Lake Nipissing.

For the second area of interest, turn left after crossing the stream to see an area of recent dunes. Past these lies limestone bedrock carved into glacial flutes. Behind the dunes is a fabulous fen where insectivorous sundews and pitcher plants can be found. A good time to visit the fen is in the spring, when orchids proliferate. Beyond the fen is a coniferous forest.

The third option is to head for the open rocky shoreline extending from Singing Sands past the end of the reserve. Scattered with glacial flutes and cobble beaches, the area is home for many wildflowers.

Take the winding journey back out to Highway 6 via the long route by continuing around Dorcas Bay and heading south beside Whiskey Marsh and Still Marsh, sometimes hugging the lakeshore. This road eventually turns to the east, skirts Scugog Lake and connects to Highway 6. Should you wish to continue to Manitoulin, described in the next chapter, we suggest you head back to Tobermory for the ferry.

above Niagara Falls and disappeared on her maiden voyage about 1679.

Perhaps the most famous of the islands is Flowerpot. You may think the flowerpots were created by elemental forces—wind, water, cold, heat—sapping the softer underlayers while the hard dolostone caps totter in defiance of physics. But the Ojibwa believed otherwise. The flowerpots were lovers from separate nations and so forbidden to each other. Like most lovers, they weren't to be denied and they ran away. The young woman's father followed, and her lover, determined to protect her, pushed on across the bay. Wind blew them off course, causing them to touch upon the forbidden island known as Island of the Caves. Desperate, the couple prayed to the manitous for forgiveness for treading on hallowed ground. The manitous, unappeased, turned the lovers into rock—the flowerpots you see today.

Mindemoya Lake

THE FRESHWATER ARCHIPELAGO

Manitoulin is the largest freshwater island in the world, dotted by lakes and two waterfalls. It is so large that the Isle of Wight and Channel Islands together would equal its size. It is, in fact, an extension of the archipelago that begins off Tobermory and includes hundreds of islands.

This is the most northerly extreme of the escarpment. It is not always easily visible, because it's not as high as other areas and much is still submerged. It seems to end somewhere before the La Cloche Mountains on the north shore of Huron, though the mountains themselves are largely sedimentary rock that abruptly changes to Precambrian Shield.

The terrain here is varied, sometimes level, sometimes rolling, sometimes stony, sometimes sandy. It is a fascinating region, full of hidden secrets, both cultural and geological. In many places the rock lies exposed by cuts. You will notice the extreme softness of it, the way it crumbles so easily. In other places the dolostone predominates and forms hard, almost shining, exposures.

Looking out to Campbell Bay from Indian Point Bridge

10

Manitoulin—Island of Gitche Manitou

Once you leave the ferry at Manitoulin Island, you tred on hallowed ground. Called Manitouminis, the home of Gitche Manitou, by the Ojibwa, this scape of rock and wind and trees where manitous dwelled would not yield to the plough or settlement.

This was also where the legendary *maymayquayshi* landed their stone canoes. *Maymayquayshi* were magical, powerful people, no taller than three feet, covered in auburn fur, regularly sighted by the Ojibwa. Like most manitous, however, they fell silent with the advent of settlers in the 1860s.

Manitoulin is the site of the largest unceded native reserve in North America, Wikwemikong.

Retaining control of their sacred land wasn't easy for the Ojibwa. The British Crown wanted Manitoulin, and in 1863, six special constables were sent from Toronto, with six from Barrie and eight from Collingwood, to stop 400 Ojibwa engaged in revolt. Arrests and charges were made. An editor of *The Globe and Mail* wrote: "Because the Indians are not willing that the whites should occupy their island, are these subjects of the Queen to be driven out of her dominions by violence? Thousands of Indians have with their blood, sealed their loyalty to the British Crown!"

Unlike elsewhere along the escarpment, settlers were not the first whites to move in—oil merchants were. As early as 1864, requests to lease massive areas near Wikwemikong were put before the government. Surprisingly, the Jesuits, active on the peninsula, advised that the Ojibwa should decide whether to lease and be responsible for the collection of any revenue. The government nevertheless issued leases, the only concession to the Ojibwa being that all employment had to be from the native pool. By September 1866, more than 3,642 hectares (9,000 acres) on the northern half of the Wikwemikong peninsula were leased.

Only two companies—Lake Huron Oil Company and Great Manitoulin—managed to drill. By 1869, both had ceased operation.

The attempt at agricultural settlement was disastrous. According to the treaty, the Ojibwa were to have been given first choice of land. Theirs was a hunter-gatherer tradition; families came together in villages during the summer months and dispersed to hunting grounds in winter, so opinion was divided about making a permanent arrangement. When lands came up for white purchase in June 1866, the band at Little Current was in favour of smaller, scattered reserves which would have emulated their former settlements.

With this matter in limbo, settlers began their purchase of lands. In the following seven years 14,378 hectares (38,000 acres) were sold. Distance from southern markets and shipping difficulties were probably the main factors in poor sales.

A slow and methodical rape of the land ensued. Sugar bush was tapped to the point of depletion and forests were stripped. By the 1880s, with cleared lands still available for agriculture, the settlers began to arrive in larger numbers.

The maple stands grew on rocky, thin soil, so settlers turned to the softwood lowlands, putting them to the match to expose the rich muck to the sun. Once dried, these soils produced abundant harvests of wheat and other cereals. Not only were the forests destroyed, but the wetlands as well. By the turn of the century almost half of Manitoulin was logged out.

With farms prospering, the need for roads increased. Once the roads came in, post offices appeared. The railway was brought in, and the shipping trade thrived, supported by an active fish industry.

But the boom died by the 1930s: the forests were depleted; the waters had been overfished and were infested with lamprey, further endangering existing stock. Tourism became Manitoulin's principal industry.

To cover Manitoulin you'll need four to five days.

We begin our tour at South Baymouth, which can be reached from the south by ferry from Tobermory, or from the north by Highway 6.

Originally known as Sagradawangog, South Baymouth is a terminal town for the Tobermory ferry. Try visiting the

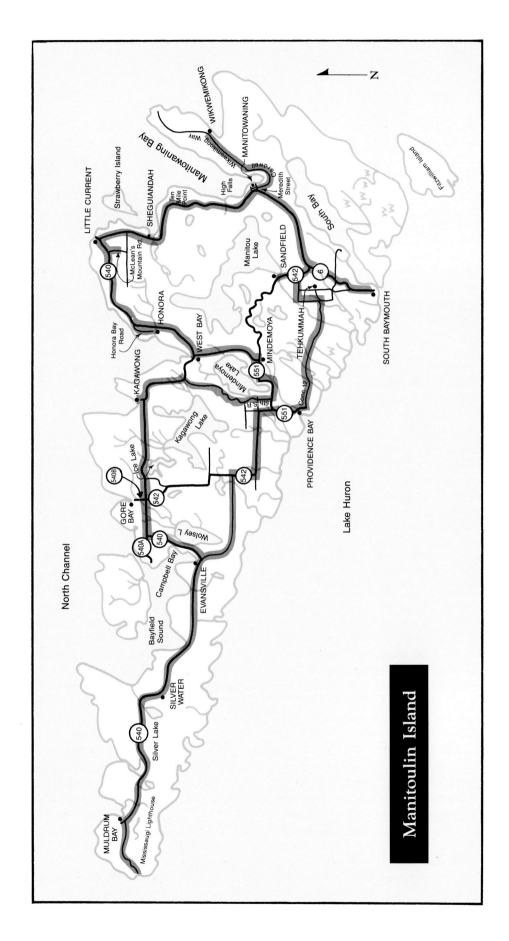

Manitoulin Island

Little Schoolhouse and Museum, which covers local history, and an excellent gallery just off the beaten track, displaying works by local artists.

A bus tour of the island is offered through Manitoulin Travel. You can choose between two loops, one to the east, one to the west. The bus runs during July and August only, from 1:15 p.m. to 5:15 p.m., Monday to Saturday. Information can be obtained at the Ontario Northland terminal at harbourside, or you can call. Manitoulin Travel is listed in For Further Information.

Head north out of South Baymouth on Highway 6, through farmland. Continue on Highway 6 to Meredith Street. Turn right. At the forks, keep to the right, to Cardwell Street.

Our journey takes us around Manitowaning Bay, with a fine view, through the villages of Two O'Clock and Buzwah and from there into Wikwemikong. After some distance Cardwell Street becomes Wikwemikong Way.

Wikwemikong

The eastern peninsula, where Wikwemikong Reserve is situated, is home to 3,000 Ojibwa and encompasses 1,214 hectares (3,000 acres). The name Wikwemikong means "home of the beaver."

The largest of the Jesuit missions was established here, in the seventeenth century, and it's still active. The ruins are limestone, probably quarried from the escarpment, located adjacent to the existing Catholic church.

Perhaps one of the best times to visit Wikwemikong is during the Wikwemikong Pow Wow held Civic Holiday weekend (the first weekend in August), attracting dancers from the Canadian West and the American Southwest.

Head back along Wikwemikong Way to Arthur Street and turn right.

Manitowaning

A refurbished nineteenth-century grist mill, and the *M. V. Norisle*, one of the old Great Lakes ferry boats, are attractions. The Assiginack Museum, named for the famed Chief Blackbird, is also well worth a visit. St. Paul's Anglican, built in 1847, is the oldest church building in Northern Ontario. Swimming, public washrooms and a change house are also available. An annual fair is held in August.

When entering Manitowaning from Arthur Street, watch for a historical plaque and sign to the left, indicating the Manitowaning Treaties and Assiginack Museum respectively. After visiting the museum, continue on Arthur Street and turn right at Queen Street. This will take you to the harbour to visit the *Norisle*, Manitoulin Roller Mills and Burns' Wharf.

Return to Highway 6 and continue north. Just a little past Manitowaning is High Falls, which cascades directly to the right of the road. The waterfall is most admirable in spring when the creek is high. It descends into a limestone gorge and then into Manitowaning Bay. There is a picnic area here and parking facilities.

Still heading north on Highway 6, make another stop at Ten Mile Point, on the right.

Ten Mile Point

Stop at Ten Mile Point and take a spectacular view of 1,600 square kilometres (617 square miles) of blue bay. The La Cloche Mountains are in the distance. This is also the site of an early Jesuit mission, marked by a historical plaque. Ten Mile Point Trading Post is filled with art and artifacts from many of the leading native artists, Leiland Bell among them, and there is much Iroquois art.

Go north on Highway 6, bypassing Sheguiandah, and head for the Little Current and Howland Museum, situated on the right of the road.

Little Current and Howland Museum

The museum comprises log houses, an implement barn, a blacksmith's and main display, as well as a replica of a nineteenth-century water-powered grist mill. Picnic facilities are available in the park overlooking Sheguiandah Bay. Camping sites are nearby, and there is a sandy beach for swimmers or sun worshippers.

Again head north on Highway 6 into Little Current. As you go, take in the fabulous view to the left.

Little Current

Once known as Waubeiewung—"where the waters flow"— by natives, and as Le Petit Courant by voyageurs, the spot is now called Little Current. The channel current flows from east to west and back again, through a narrow passage.

Primarily a channel harbour, Little Current was a shipping site for coal through the CPR. The coal industry declined, but ships still pick up iron pellets and other northern mine products from the town.

The swinging bridge closes to land traffic for 15 minutes every hour on the hour, allowing boats to pass through the channel. It was constructed prior to the First World War.

You might want to visit Little Current during Civic Holiday for Haweater Weekend. The Haweaters were early Manitoulin settlers who staved off starvation by eating the bitter berries of the hawthorn tree. Today, the designation Haweater means one born on Manitoulin.

High Falls

Little Current-Howland Museum

Make a left at the stop sign at Highway 6 in Little Current. At the next stop, turn left onto Highway 540, following the signs to Gore Bay. At McLean's Mountain Road, turn left.

McLean's Mountain

Rising 327 metres (1,075 feet) above sea level, this section of the escarpment provides a spectacular view in almost every direction, from Honora Bay to Sheguiandah and out across the North Channel.

Continue west on Highway 540. At Honora Bay Road, turn right. The road is gravel and later becomes paved. This takes you into the village of Honora. In the bay of Honora is one of the largest cuts left by Gitche Manitou's ice knives. The settlement is picturesque, surrounded by birch-covered ridges.

Backtrack to Highway 540, and turn right. West along the road you'll see a well-marked trail to the right for Cup and Saucer Bluff.

Cup and Saucer Bluff

The cup is the little hill, which sits on the saucer, the big hill below. A trail climbs the heights to a level, grassy area. At the top, marked Adventure Trail, is an optional trail going up and down ladders to a natural rock chimney and along a narrow ledge.

Head west again on Highway 540 into the village of West Bay.

West Bay

Once called Mitchigiging—"place of the fish harpoon"—West Bay is an Ojibwa reserve and home of the Ojibwe Cultural Foundation and Gallery, and Kasheese Studios. The cultural centre provides support for native people, as well as an artistic outlet. Kasheese Studios, at the junction of Highways 540 and 551, is a gallery displaying excellent native art in many forms.

West Bay is also the site of a Jesuit mission, Church of the Immaculate Conception. It was designed with the native people in mind, emulating a traditional fire-pit meeting place, built in a 12-sided shape with two-thirds of its interior height below ground level, forming an amphitheatre.

Turn right in West Bay onto Highway 551 and head south to skirt Mindemoya Lake.

Mindemoya Lake

Long ago the wife of a chief ruined an elixir he had created for a council meeting. Her carelessness angered him so greatly that he kicked her off a cliff, and it's said she landed on her hands and knees in the water, becoming an island.

Mindemoya is probably the most beautiful of Manitoulin's lakes. Even in the days of settlers, the lake shone like an opal, shimmering in blues and greens and surrounded in crenellated white limestone abundant with caves. The lake was then and is now rich in whitefish.

Continue on Highway 551 through the village of Mindemoya. At Highway 542 West, turn right, and then right again at the 5th Sideroad. The road will take you out to Rock Garden Terrace Resort and Mindemoya Cave. Notice the alvars along the way.

Mindemoya Cave

About midway on the western shore of Mindemoya Lake is the Rock Garden Terrace Resort. The cave here was created by an ancient stream after the last glaciation. Approximately 22 metres (75 feet) deep, it has several small passages not open to the public.

The cave was discovered by three Mennonite preachers while hunting in 1888. Inside they found seven skeletons said to have been those of some Ottawa who had hidden in the cave to escape attacking Iroquois. After the remains were shipped to the Royal Ontario Museum, the museum suffered a fire and the skeletons were destroyed. Today, there is a display in the cave, portraying an aboriginal family, as well as a skeleton to represent the original discovery.

There is admission.

Continue along the 5th Sideroad. A trail marked Carnarvon-Billings Line, on the right side of the road, is available to those who wish to take a 2.5-kilometre (1.5-mile) hike along the west shore of Mindemoya Lake on old logging roads, rising through rich hardwoods. At the top is a flat dolomite plain. This is a fabulous hike in the fall.

Continue north on Sideroad 5 and turn left at the T intersection. At the next T intersection, turn left onto Highway 540 and continue into Kagawong.

Kagawong

Kagawong—"where the mists rise from the falling water"—is also called Bridal Veil Falls. To reach the falls, hike along the trail so marked.

A generating station here once supplied power to Manitoulin Island. There are picnic facilities with barbecue pits, tables and public tennis courts. Swimming is also available at the public beach.

Previously a pulp and logging port, the town is now a tourist attraction. Be sure to see the Anglican church, a well-preserved building from the turn of the century. The pulpit

Pioneer barn amid maples, Meldrum Bay

was constructed from the timber of an old wrecked ship. Kagawong also has a lighthouse.

Continue west along Highway 540. At the stop sign, turn right into Gore Bay.

Gore Bay

Pushkdinong—"the barren hill"—has evolved into Gore Bay, a town tucked into the fabulous cliffs that wrap round it like wings. No longer barren, the hill is grown over with trees. Gore Bay is a great place for shopping and tearooms and is the government seat of Manitoulin District.

The Gore Bay Museum is in an old jailhouse and jail-keeper's home.

To tour part of the town, turn right on Hall Street and climb the bluff. Keep left until you reach the Harold Noble Memorial Lookout. You'll be rewarded with a view of Gore Bay and the escarpment. There are picnic tables here.

Descend again to Gore Bay and follow the signs to the museum. It is well posted. A tearoom and a gallery are located at the lakeside.

Backtrack to Highway 540 and turn right. Turn left, where 540 continues, and cross Indian Point Bridge. Lake Wolsely was originally separated from Georgian Bay by a mile of shallow reef. Indian Point Bridge now spans the distance.

Continue along Highway 540, through Fernlee, Silver Water and around Silver Lake. At Silver Lake is a picnic area with a good beach. A pre-dawn visit and much patience and perseverance will reward you. Deer frequently visit the lake in large numbers. The beach is peppered with their footprints.

Continue west along Highway 540, which runs directly into the village of Meldrum Bay, one of our favourite spots simply because it's so quiet.

Meldrum Bay

This is the western entrance to Manitoulin, a picturesque former fishing village. The Net Shed Museum is situated on the waterfront, displaying trapper, voyageur, farm and fishing collections. There is also a lighthouse.

Backtrack along Highway 540 to the Mississaugi Lighthouse marker. Turn right. Should you be visiting in off season, you'll have to hike the remaining kilometre as the area will be closed.

On the way to the Mississaugi Lighthouse, you'll travel through one of the largest remaining stands of timber on Manitoulin. There's also a bird sanctuary on the left of the road. Remote and beautiful, the land around Mississaugi Lighthouse has excellent camping facilities. The lighthouse itself is a historic attraction.

Backtrack to Highway 540 and turn right. In Evansville, take the first right, posted as the direction to Moonbeam Camp. At the T intersection, turn left. At the next T, turn right onto Highway 542 and stay on the paved road. At Hawberry House, continue south onto Highway 551 to Providence Bay.

Providence Bay

The largest sand beach on the island is here in the place the Ojibwa called Bebekodawangog—"where sand curves around the water." This is an ancient Ojibwa summer village site. Picnic tables are available at the beach.

Continue out of Providence Bay, past the beach to the government docks. On the left is Concession 12, a lovely rural drive, especially in the fall.

Just before the Manitou River is a trail marker for the Carnarvon-Tehkummah Trail, to the right.

Carnarvon-Tehkummah Trail

A 2.5-kilometre (1.5-mile) hike, the trail skirts Michael Bay, passing through spruce-balsam lowlands. It can be wet, so we recommend hiking boots.

Continue east along Concession 12 and cross the Manitou River. At the T intersection, turn left onto the 10th Sideroad. Follow the pavement around to the right. The pavement ends and becomes a gravel road into the village of Tehkummah, named for Louis Tehkummah, the great chief whose name meant "rays of light flashing in the sky."

Continue out of Tehkummah along the gravel road, which becomes 542A. At the intersection, turn left onto 542 West, towards Sandfield and the fish hatchery.

Sandfield Fish Hatchery and Manitou Lake

The largest lake on the island is said to have been the home of Gitche Manitou. The Ministry of Natural Resources' Sandfield Fish Hatchery is on the left as you enter the village. It is open to the public.

Backtrack along 542 to the intersection of Highway 6. Turn right and return to South Baymouth.

And so we end our tour of the Niagara Escarpment. We hope exploring this unique part of Ontario, rich in both natural and cultural history, brings you adventure and the pleasure of discovery. If you have been touched by the experience, as we were, we challenge you to help preserve the vulnerable and invaluable escarpment environment.

For Further Information

Bruce Peninsula National Park, Box 189, Tobermory, Ontario N0H 2R0   (519) 596-2233

Bruce Trail Association, P.O. Box 857, Hamilton, Ontario L8N 3N9

Chippewas of Nawash, Band Office, R.R. 5, Wiarton, Ontario N0H 2T0   (519) 534-1689

Crawford Lake Conservation Area, Burlington, Ontario (416) 854-0234 (see Halton Region Conservation Authority for mailing address)

Credit Valley Conservation Authority, 1255 Derry Road West, Meadowvale, Ontario L5N 6R4   1 (800) 668-5557,   (416) 670-1615

Double Deck Tours Ltd., 3957 Bossert Road, R.R. #3, Niagara Falls, Ontario L2E 6S6   (416) 295-3051

Dundas Historical Society Museum, Dundas, Ontario (416) 627-7412 (telephone information only)

Dundurn Castle, Dundurn Park, York Boulevard, Hamilton, Ontario L8R 3H1   (416) 522-5313

Fathom Five National Marine Park, Box 189, Tobermory, Ontario N0H 2R0   (519) 596-2510

Federation of Ontario Naturalists, 335 Lesmill Road, Don Mills, Ontario M3B 2W8   (416) 444-8419

Festival Country Travel Association, 38 Darling Street, Suite 102, Brantford, Ontario N3T 6A8   (519) 756-3230

Georgian Lakelands Travel Association, Dept T88, P.O. Box 39, 66 Coldwater Street East, Orillia, Ontario L3V 6H9   (705) 325-7160

Grey-Sauble Conservation Authority, R.R. #4, Owen Sound, Ontario N4K 5N6   (519) 376-3076

Halton Region Conservation Authority, P.O. Box 1097, Station B, Burlington, Ontario L7P 3S9   (416) 336-1158

Hamilton-Wentworth Conservation Authority, P.O. Box 7099, Ancaster, Ontario   (416) 525-2181

Hilton Falls Conservation Area, Milton, Ontario (416) 854-0262 (telephone information only)

Jordan Historical Museum of the Twenty, Box 39, Jordan, Ontario L0R 1S0   (416) 562-5242

Laura Secord Homestead, Queenston, Ontario (416) 262-4851 (telephone information only)

Lundy's Lane Historical Museum, 5810 Ferry Street, Niagara Falls, Ontario L2G 1S9   (416) 358-5082

Maid of the Mist, 5920 River Road, P.O. Box 808, Niagara Falls, Ontario L2E 6V6   (416) 358-5781

Manitoulin Tourist Association, P.O. Box 119, Little Current, Ontario P0P 1K0   (705) 368-3021

Manitoulin Travel, Gore Bay, Ontario   (705) 282-2848 (telephone information only)

Ministry of Natural Resources, Grey/Bruce, 611 Ninth Avenue East, Owen Sound, Ontario M4K 3E4   1 (800) 265-3720,   (519) 376-3860

Ministry of Natural Resources, Maple District, P.O. Box 7400, 10401 Dufferin Street, Maple, Ontario L6A 1S9   (416) 832-2761

Ministry of Natural Resources, Niagara Peninsula Region, P.O. Box 1070, Fonthill, Ontario L0S 1E0 (416) 892-2656

Niagara Escarpment Commission, 232 Guelph Street, Georgetown, Ontario L7G 4B1   (416) 877-5191

Niagara Falls Parks Commission, Box 150, Niagara Falls, Ontario L2E 6T2   (416) 356-2241

Niagara Peninsula Conservation Authority, Centre Street, Allanburg, Ontario L0S 1A0   (416) 227-1013

Nottawasaga Conservation Authority, R.R. #1, Angus, Ontario L0M 1B0   (705) 424-1479

Ojibwe Cultural Foundation and Gallery, Excelsior Post Office, West Bay, Ontario P0P 1G0   (705) 377-4902

Ontario Agricultural Museum, Milton, Ontario (416) 878-8151 (telephone information only)

Ontario Northland Marine Services, (M.S. *Chi-Cheemaun* and M.S. *Nindeweyma*) Tobermory Terminal (519) 596-2510, South Baymouth Terminal (705) 859-3161 or toll free at 1 (800) 265-3163

Rainbow Country Travel Association, R.R. #3, Site 14, Box 29, Sudbury, Ontario P3E 4N1

Rattlesnake Point Conservation Area, Milton, Ontario (416) 878-1147 (see Halton Region Conservation Authority for mailing address)

Royal Botanical Gardens, Box 399, Hamilton, Ontario L8N 3H8   (416) 527-1158, toll free in 416 area code   1 (800) 263-8450

Scenic Caves and Caverns, Box 558, Collingwood, Ontario L9Y 4B2   (705) 445-2828

St. Catharines Historical Museum, 343 Merritt Street, St. Catharines, Ontario L2T 1K7   (416) 227-2962

Terra Cotta Conservation Area, Terra Cotta, Ontario (416) 877-9650 (for mailing address see Credit Valley Conservation Authority)

Welland Historical Museum, Welland, Ontario (416) 732-2215 (telephone information only)

Bibliography

Ancaster Township Historical Society. *Ancaster's Heritage*. Ancaster, 1970.

Beaumont, Ralph. *Alton, A Pictorial History*. Erin, Ontario: The Boston Mills Press, 1974.

———. *Cataract and the Forks of the Credit, A Pictorial History*. Erin, Ontario: The Boston Mills Press, 1974.

———, and James Filby. *The Great Horseshoe Wreck*. Erin, Ontario: The Boston Mills Press, 1974.

Bell, Alexander C. *Crawford Lake Conservation Area Master Plan*. Halton Region Conservation Authority, June 1978.

———. *Hilton Falls Master Plan*. Halton Region Conservation Authority, July 1982.

Brooksbank, Jack. *The Hockley Story*. Hockley Village: Jacques Bea Studios, 1988.

Brownell, Vivian R. *A Life Science Inventory and Evaluation of the Nottawasaga Lookout Study Area*. Ministry of Natural Resources, 1980.

Bruce Trail Association, The. *The Bruce Trail Guidebook*. Fifteenth Edition, 1985.

Campbell, Marjorie Freeman. *A Mountain and a City: The Story of Hamilton*. Toronto: McClelland and Stewart Limited, 1966.

Carnochan, Janet, and William Briggs. *History of Niagara*, 1914.

Chippewas of Nawash Education Department. *The History of Cape Croker*, 1980.

Cook, William E. *History of Inglewood*. Erin, Ontario: The Boston Mills Press, 1975.

Croft, Melba Morris. *Tall Tales and Legends of Georgian Bay*.

Davidson, T. Arthur. *A New History of Grey County*. The Grey County Historical Society, 1972.

Dimitroff, T.C. *The Portage Era in Queenston*. Brock University, 1968.

Donaldson, Gordon. *Niagara! The Eternal Circus*. Toronto: Doubleday Canada Limited, 1979.

Dufferin County. *Dufferin County Centennial 1881–1981*. 1981.

Duguid, Robert E., and David Morgan. *Rattlesnake Point Conservation Area Master Plan*. Halton Region Conservation Authority, September 1983.

Emery, Claire, and Barbara Ford. *From Pathway to Skyway: A History of Burlington*. Confederation Centennial Committee of Burlington, 1967.

Federation of Ontario Naturalists. *Seasons*.

Filby, James. *Credit Valley Railway*. Erin, Ontario: The Boston Mills Press, 1974.

———. *The Road to Boston Mills*. Erin, Ontario: The Boston Mills Press, 1976.

Fonthill Women's Institute. *History of the Village of Fonthill*. 1963.

Halliday, Larry and Kathy. *About Dunedin*. Dunedin.

Hutton, Jack, David Wootton, Barbara Guyatt, and Gayle Hall. *Ball's Falls Conservation Area Master Plan*. Niagara Peninsula Conservation Authority, May 1980.

Jackson, John N. *St. Catharines, Ontario, Its Early Years*. Mika Publishing Company, 1976.

Kelling, Elizabeth Anne. *The Roots of Amaranth*. Erin, Ontario: The Boston Mills Press, 1981.

Leitch, Adelaide. *Into the High Country*. Corporation of the County of Dufferin.

M.M. Dillon Limited and D.W. Graham and Associations Limited. *Boyne Valley Provincial Park*. Ministry of Natural Resources.

Marion, Nola, and Barbara Guyatt. *St. John's Conservation Area Master Plan*. Niagara Peninsula Conservation Authority, July 1980.

McDonald, John. *Halton Sketches*. Dills Printing and Publishing Company Limited, 1976.

McMillan, C. J. *Early History of the Township of Erin*. Erin, Ontario: The Boston Mills Press, 1974.

Ministry of Natural Resources. *Bognor Marsh Management Area Master Plan*.

———. *Bruce's Caves Conservation Area Master Plan*.

———. *Colpoy's Range and Lookout Conservation Area Master Plan*.

———. *Craigleith Provincial Park Master Plan*.

———. *Devil's Glen Provincial Park Management Plan Background Information*. 1985.

———. *Epping Lookout Master Plan*.

———. *Forks of the Credit Provincial Park Master Plan*. 1989.

———. *The Glen Management Area Master Plan*.

———. *Griersville Escarpment Properties Master Plan*.

———. *Inglis Falls Conservation Area Master Plan*.

———. *Kemble Mountain Management Area Master Plan*.

———. *Lavender Falls Candidate Provincial Park Interim Management Statement*, 1986.

———. *Lindenwood Management Area Master Plan.*

———. *Mono Cliffs Provincial Park Master Plan.* 1974.

———. *Old Baldy Conservation Area Master Plan.*

———. *Pottawatomi Conservation Area Master Plan.*

———. *Red Bay Nature Preserve Master Plan.*

———. *Rocklyn Creek Properties Master Plan.*

———. *Scott's Falls Interim Management Statement,* 1986.

———. *Skinner Bluffs Management Area Master Plan.*

———. *Slough of Despond Management Area Master Plan.*

———. *St. Jean's Point Nature Preserve Master Plan.*

———. *Spey River Forest East Master Plan.*

———. *Spirit Rock Conservation Area Master Plan.*

———. *Walters Creek Management Area Master Plan.*

———. *West Rocks Conservation Area Master Plan.*

Nelles, Frank. *Cheltenham: A Credit Valley Mill Town.* Erin, Ontario: The Boston Mills Press, 1975.

Niagara Escarpment Commission. *Cuesta Publications.*

Niagara-on-the-Lake, A Quaint Community at the Mouth of the Niagara River. Niagara Advance, 1971.

Nottawasaga Conservation Authority. *Petun Conservation Area Master Plan.*

A Pictorial History of Erin Village. Erin, Ontario: The Boston Mills Press, 1980.

Poirier, Marie, and Gayle Hall. *Woodend Conservation Area Master Plan.* Niagara Peninsula Conservation Authority, September 1981.

Read, Allan A. *Unto the Hills: A History of the Parish of East Mono,* 1952.

Reid, Elmer. *Mulmur, More of the Township's Story.* The Mulmur Township Library Board, 1981.

Richardson, William G. *The Story of Whittington.*

Saunders, Kathleen. *Saunders' History of Georgetown.* Erin, Ontario: The Boston Mills Press, 1976.

Sawden, Stephen. *History of Dufferin County.*

Stoney Creek, the Corporation of the Town of. *Saltfleet Then and Now.* 1975.

Switzer, Neil T. *Crawford Conservation Complex Master Plan.* Halton Region Conservation Authority, July 1986.

Corporation of the County of Peel, The. *A History of Peel County to Mark Its Centenary.* 1967.

Tovell, Walter M. *The Niagara Escarpment.* Toronto: University of Toronto Press, 1965.

Trimble, Bernice. *Belfountain, Caves, Castles and Quarries in the Caledon Hills.* Belfountain-Rockside Women's Institute, 1975.

Waterdown East Flamborough Centennial Committee. *Waterdown and East Flamborough, 1867–1967.* 1967.

Weaver, Emily P. *The Counties of Ontario.* Bell and Cockburn, 1913.

White, Kelly, and Gayle Hall. *Beamer Memorial Conservation Area, Louth Conservation Area, Mountainview Conservation Area, Rockway Conservation Area, Woolverton Conservation Area Master Plan.* Niagara Peninsula Conservation Authority, September 1982.

Whiteside, Margaret. *Belfountain and the Tubtown Pioneers.* Erin, Ontario: The Boston Mills Press, 1975.

Wightman, W.R. *Forever on the Fringe.* Toronto: University of Toronto Press, 1982.

Woodhouse, Roy T. *A Short History of Dundas.* Town of Dundas, 1947.

Zatyko, Mary. *Terra Cotta, A Capsule History.* Erin, Ontario: The Boston Mills Press, 1979.